GOLDE'S HOMEMADE COOKIES

OVER 130 DELICIOUS
AND ORIGINAL RECIPES

GOLDE HOFFMAN SOLOWAY

Illustrated by Loretta Trezzo

GRAMERCY BOOKS
NEW YORK

Special thanks to Harriet Patrick and Peg Blanchette for their assistance and enthusiastic support in bringing this project to completion.

With appreciation to Rachel Hutchins and Linda Luxenberg for all their help.

Notice: The information contained in this book is true, complete, and accurate to the best of our knowledge. All recommendations and suggestions are made without any guarantees on the part of the author or publisher. The author and publisher disclaim all liability incurred in connection with the use of this information.

This 2004 edition is published by Gramercy Books, an imprint of Random House Value Publishing, a division of Random House, Inc., New York, by arrangement with Williamson Publishing Co.

Gramercy is a registered trademark and the colophon is a trademark of Random House, Inc.

Random House
New York • Toronto • London • Sydney • Auckland
www.randomhouse.com

Interior design: Trezzo-Braren Studio
Illustrations: Loretta Trezzo
Typography: Villanti & Sons, Printers, Inc.

Printed and bound in the United States

Library of Congress Cataloging-in-Publication Data

Soloway, Golde Hoffman.
    Golde's homemade cookies : over 130 delicious and original recipes / Golde Hoffman Soloway ; illustrated by Loretta Trezzo.
        p. cm.
    Originally published: Expanded ed. Charlotte, Vt. : Williamson Pub. Co., c1990.
    Includes index.
    ISBN 0-517-22284-1
      1. Cookies. I. Title.

TX772.S67 2004
641.8'654—dc22

2003056841

10 9 8 7 6 5 4 3

Contents

DEDICATION

For David.

ACKNOWLEDGEMENTS

With abundant thanks . . .

To all the wonderful people who have shared recipes with me over these many years.

To my family and friends who have gathered around our table for coffee, tea, cookies and good conversation.

To Susan Williamson for her editorial assistance, to Jack Williamson for his enthusiastic delight in this book, to Loretta Trezzo for her beautiful illustrations and book design.

And to my grandchildren – Rachel, Daniel, Sarah, Zachary, Joelle, Jonathan, and David.

A Message from Golde

It's been six years since I wrote the first edition of *Golde's Homemade Cookies*. What began as a favor to my daughter and son-in-law (a true labor of love as I tested and retested every recipe, no matter how many times I had baked it before) turned into a wonderful surprise. Believe me, I never dreamed my book of favorite cookie recipes would sell over 50,000 copies!

What it brought me was an embarrassment of riches – not the monetary kind because at my age I know better than to measure happiness or success that way. The riches and joy came in the form of hundreds upon hundreds of letters from readers the world over. I wish I could share with each of you the warmth of human nature that I discovered in the short notes and long letters sent my way. Somehow this cookie cookbook transcended the usual barriers and irritations of everyday life, and people felt moved to write me about their favorite cookie experiences, about their children and grandchildren, about their aches and pains, and joys and sorrows. Yes, I have many newfound friends. It's been an uplifting experience I wish I could share with all of you. People are good and caring and responsive.

This new expanded edition came about as a result of many requests. I'd bake an unusual cookie and people would ask if they could find the recipe in my book. Or I'd bring out an old favorite that somehow got overlooked the first time around, and there would be a chorus of, "Why did you leave this one out? It's my favorite." (My son-in-law, Stanley, claims *every* recipe is his favorite – at least while he's eating it.)

And so this new edition evolved with many new-found favorites that family, friends, neighbors and letter-writers urged me to share with all of you. So, dear friends, cookie bakers, and cookie eaters, sample these treats, bake with your children and grandchildren, send a batch of thoughtfulness to someone who needs cheering, and most of all . . . enjoy!

"Will you please send me two more copies of Golde's Homemade Cookies. *I've enjoyed my copy so much—have read it cover to cover. The printing is great—the art work is delightful. All in all, it is a 'happy' book to own."*

Mrs. E. Mellish
New York

"After reading the article about Golde Soloway in Yankee *magazine and then baking all the recipes given, I have decided that I can't live without her book."*

M. Kahle
Illinois

"I am a midwesterner who has discovered Golde's Homemade Cookies *through* Yankee *magazine. Please, please, would love to have her cookbook."*

S. Dunne
Texas

"Many years ago I was a next door neighbor of Golde and David in Jasper. Little did I think then that I'd be able to look back and say, 'I knew her when . . .'"

F. Elliott
New York

"The best part of a week-end vacation was buying your delicious cookie cookbook. Don't stop with cookies—I'd love a dessert cookbook, too!"

E. Sabin
Montreal

"I'm enjoying my cookie book so much that I'm buying some more to give as gifts."

J. Smith
Kentucky

"I have a Golde's Homemade Cookies book. I love it. My friend would also like one . . ."

J. Diana
Pennsylvania

"Please send me Golde's Homemade Cookies. I was so delighted with this book (ordered last December) that I want to get another for my daughter-in-law."

J. Fox
New Mexico

"I have a copy of Golde's book and have enjoyed it greatly. My daughter has specified that that's what she wants for Christmas! Thanks to Golde."

M. Coleman
Washington

"Your cookie book reminds me what my mother made years ago. And I am 80 years old now."

M. Kenney
Ohio

"What I particularly enjoy is the large print and the fact that there is only one recipe per page."

L. Cook
Virginia

"Please send 3 copies of Golde's Homemade Cookies. We just read about it in Yankee magazine and made cookies all morning. They are great."

> **B. Moore**
> **Washington**

"After having made several of your recipes I feel comfortable enough to call you by your first name. Congratulations and many thanks from my satisfied taste buds."

> **J. Rhodes**
> **Connecticut**

"Having tried—and drooled in the process—Golde Soloway's cookies which appeared in Yankee, I hastily enclose my check."

> **L. Cowan**
> **Florida**

"I take the liberty of referring to you as 'Dear' as we both like to bake cookies for our grandchildren, because our 'pie crusts never turn out.' "

> **M. Aleardi**
> **New Jersey**

"The recipes are the first cookie recipes I have tried that worked right the first time!"

> **J. McQueen**
> **Pennsylvania**

Introduction

People often ask how I got so involved in cookie-baking. My answer is always the same, uninspired as it might seem; I bake cookies because in the time it takes to bake one cake, I can bake dozens of cookies, and, I must admit, because my pie crusts never quite measure up to my friends' and neighbors'.

My daughters, who are into the psychological meaning of such things, tell me that my cookies are my personal expression of love and caring. And there is some truth to that for cookies were always my way of celebrating the joy of family, friends and neighbors at weddings, Bar Mitzvahs, graduations, holidays, anniversaries, and impromptu get-togethers; in fact, just about any happy occasion. And, too, I find I send cookies to help ease the burden during painful events in the lives of the people close to me.

Then there is this a-little-something-for-the-trip-home habit – I think it started when my eldest daughter went to college – of sending cookies home with house guests. (Invariably, I always hear how the cookies are all gone before they reach their destination.) And, of course, I bring tins of cookies whenever I go off for a visit; now that I know most friends' favorites, I try to take those along, always mixed with something new that I'm trying.

So I guess my daughters are right. Cookies are my way of saying to someone that they are special – right down to their favorite kinds of cookies. And it does give me pleasure to see my family and friends brighten up and say, "Ah, good! Some of Golde's cookies!"

HOMEMADE IS BETTER

In this age of fast food and instant satisfaction, it gets harder and harder to justify some of the time-consuming methods, or as my grandchildren say, "olden times" ways of doing things.

Not so, with homebaked cookies. Plain and simply, homebaked cookies *taste* much better than anything you can buy. There is really no comparison with store-bought cookies. Actually, the packaged varieties don't even deserve to be called "cookies," and the only ones I buy are from the Girl Scouts (still the best chocolate cookie mints anywhere). Bakeries in supermarkets and in malls don't really come close to homebaked cookies either.

Actually, I think any cookie should be considered suspect if it is surrounded by perfectly shaped, perfectly browned, perfectly *perfect* identical cookies. Give me a good batch of homemade *individuality* anytime, fresh from the oven, the house filled with the aroma of mingling spices, each cookie slightly different in shape and size. They might not win any blue ribbons at the county fair and they'd never meet bakery standards in appearance, but for flavor, texture, and aroma, they're unbeatable.

FINDING THE TIME TO BAKE

Let's face it . . . free time is a thing of the past. We're all too busy, our calendars filled with meetings, appointments, and varied responsibilities. But, take another look; isn't there a small amount of time here or there, because that's all you really need, a small bit of time.

As you'll see, I've recorded preparation time for all of my recipes, and some need as little as 10–15 minutes to prepare the batter. So do that much and stick the batter in the fridge (covered with waxed paper) until later

that day when you're preparing dinner or the next day when you have another bit of spare time. Then bake that batch or two. There, you've baked some delicious cookies in time that otherwise would have been unproductive.

Basically, *fit your cookie-baking into the rhythm of your lifestyle*, rather than planning your day around cookie-baking time. When you have the time, bake and freeze the extras. When you don't have the time or inclination, dig into your freezer reserve.

I do most of my baking in the wee hours of the morning. If I can't sleep, I get up and make a batch or two. (It's a lot better than worrying about not sleeping.) I feel comfortable padding around the kitchen in the early sunrise hours, and my family loves awakening to the aroma of freshly baked cookies.

Most importantly, think of cookie-baking as part of your leisure time activity – relaxation rather than a chore – fun to do with friends and neighborhood children, and you'll be surprised how quickly time makes itself available.

PLAN WAY AHEAD

If you need a large number of cookies for a particular time of year or a special event, then plan way ahead. I have all of my holiday baking done three months in advance, except for some special cookies that my grandchildren like baking right around holiday time.

I always bake in the late spring so there's a freezer full of cookies for those hot summer days; this way I don't have to heat up the house with a hot oven, and I still have some special treats to go with iced tea or fresh fruit.

For my grandson's Bar Mitzvah, I baked 1,000 cookies – gradually over a three-month period. They looked delicious and tasted as fresh as if they were baked that same day. All it takes is a little careful planning, proper freezer wrapping (see chapter 1), and a big freezer (or a generous friend with a big freezer).

And I do plan a particular cookie menu depending on the event, the time of year, and who will be there. So for a brunch, I tend toward the less sweet kinds of cookies and those using fruits and nuts; for weddings, I lean toward the delicate, lighter varieties often with lemon or liqueur flavorings. For children, I go for anything with chocolate morsels, shapes, and colored sugar crystals.

BAKING WITH KIDS, PRESENTATION, PACKAGING ARE IMPORTANT

Actually I find these subjects very important indeed, so I've devoted fuller discussion of them elsewhere in this book. You'll find:

Flexibility . . . see chapter 4

Freezing . . . see chapter 1

Baking with Children . . . see chapter 5

Presentation Pointers . . . see chapter 6

COOKIES ARE ALWAYS IN STYLE

My publisher tells me that cookies are in vogue right now. I have to smile to myself as I try to think when, in my seventy-plus years, cookies have ever been out of style!

True, there are some new "in" kinds of cookies, but those never seem to replace the old favorites that are gobbled up as quickly as I set out a platterful.

I do test new recipes often, although I tend to fall back on my own personal favorites which I have been baking over the past 50 years. Force of habit, I guess.

But I don't claim to have originated many of these recipes. Oh, I've altered them, added a bit of this, a dash of that, often because that's what I happened to have on hand, and if it turned out tastier than the original recipe, why I changed it for the better. Recipes seem to go full circle, and oftentimes I'm given a "new" recipe only to find that it's one of my early ones with a catchy name.

So where did my collection of recipes come from . . . it came from Elaine, Jane, Debby, Susan, Ethel, Suny, Norine, Bev, Betty, Mildred, Syl, Helen, Peg, Gen, Florence, Jewel, Jeanne, Caroline, Merlene, Joyce, Marilyn, Mickey, Frances, the fine people who sent me their favorite recipes, the ladies from Jasper and Tarrytown, the woman on the airplane, and the one on the bus, their friends, and friends of their friends.

And they've all been baked many times over by me.

Enjoy!

CHAPTER

1

Golde's Basic Cookie How-To

Anyone can bake cookies and have them turn out well . . . most of the time! I still have batches that aren't quite right, sometimes for a recipe I've used for years. When that happens I usually blame the oven, but truthfully I don't really know what went wrong.

But with a flexible attitude, and a creative spirit, baking cookies can be one of those simple rewarding experiences.

There's no need to make a big investment in utensils. When I first started baking, I had a wood cookstove for my oven, a bowl and wooden spoon for beating the batter, and a well-used cookie sheet (which was the secret to my success). Somehow it all worked just fine.

BASIC NEEDS

- **Three cookie sheets**

Bright, heavy-gauge aluminum cookie sheets are best because they don't absorb the heat, so cookies won't burn on the bottom. If you prefer non-stick sheets, then choose light-colored ones. Have 3 so you always have one in the oven, one cooling and one to work with.

- **Timer**
- **Measuring spoons**
- **Glass measuring cups:** for liquid ingredients
- **Graduated measuring cups:** for dry ingredients
- **Wooden spoons**
- **Set of nesting bowls:** small, medium, large
- **Rubber spatula:** so no batter is wasted
- **Metal spatula:** for removing cookies from pans
- **Wire racks:** for cooling

- **Electric mix master:** not essential; a small hand-held electric mixer works fine
- **Sifter or fine sieve**
- **8- or 9-inch-square glass or metal baking pan**
- **11″ × 7″ glass or metal baking pan**
- **9″ × 13″ baking pan or 15″ × 10″ jelly-roll pan**
- **Cookie press:** needed only for a few recipes
- **Cookie cutters:** fun to collect and kids love using them, but a glass rim works fine, too
- **Rolling pin:** use a mayonnaise jar filled with water if you don't have a rolling pin

Nice but not necessary:

- **Large mix master:** works especially well on recipes where you gradually add ingredients
- **Food processor:** If you are comfortable using your food processor, then by all means, experiment with it. You can quickly process dough with a steel blade. You'll soon learn which batters mix well (especially dough-like crusts in chapter 2).
- **Nut chopper:** A small nut chopper is wonderful especially when adding finely chopped nut meats, but you can do this by hand with a wooden bowl and hand chopper, too.
- **Microwave:** Your microwave can be a great time-saver for preparation. Use it to melt butter and chocolate pieces (otherwise, use a double-boiler), warm milk and water. The microwave is also good for warming cookies to bring back that fresh-out-of-the-oven goodness, and it works wonders for refreshing almost-stale cookies.

But what the microwave does best is defrost cookies in a big hurry. Be sure to wrap them in a paper towel before reheating or defrosting.

- **Pastry blender:** Again, if you already have one, it will be very handy for many of the bar cookies in chapter 2, but you can easily manage without one.

FOLLOW THE RECIPE

The first few times I use a recipe, I follow the instructions very carefully, always measuring exactly and adding the called-for ingredients without substitutions or additions.

Then, if I feel it needs adjustments, I begin adding a little of this, deleting a little of that, until I get the recipe the way I want it. Oftentimes, I'll delete some sugar or add a little orange or lemon rind, but not until I've perfected the original recipe.

If you, too, enjoy experimenting, be sure to write down what you are trying, and don't trust your memory. There's nothing more frustrating than baking a delicious cookie and then being unable to duplicate it because you aren't quite sure what you added.

HEALTHFUL TRADE-OFFS

If you are trying to reduce the amount of sugar and salt in your diet, you can still enjoy homebaked cookies. You'll be surprised at how easy it is. Less sugar and salt won't affect the consistency of the cookies, and you'll find the natural fruit and nut flavorings are enhanced.

You may want to experiment with more natural flavorings by using grated orange or lemon peel when you reduce sugar in a recipe. Or try

adding a dash of ground cinnamon, ground nutmeg or ground ginger, or add a splash of vanilla or almond extract. And don't forget to keep abreast of new salt and sugar substitutes on the market. These products are improving and *sometimes* work in recipes, but do follow the manufacturer's recommendations as they are not interchangeable teaspoon for teaspoon with regular granulated sugar or salt.

What about some healthy trade-offs? Here are some good ideas:

- Replace white refined sugar with maple syrup, barley malt, sorghum or unsulfured molasses in the same proportions. Replace white granulated sugar with honey according to this formula: For 1 cup sugar, use ½ cup honey and decrease the liquid by ¼ cup. If there is no liquid to decrease, then increase the flour by ¼ cup. Decrease the oven temperature by 25 degrees when baking with honey because a honey batter browns quickly.
- Replace 1 cup brown sugar with ¾ cup date sugar. Or use ½ cup honey and ¼ cup date sugar.
- Increase nutrients by replacing 1 tablespoon of sugar with 1 tablespoon of unsweetened fruit juice.
- Reduce the sugar by 2-4 tablespoons and increase the vanilla or almond extract by 1 teaspoon while also increasing the ground sweet spices (nutmeg, ginger, cinnamon, cloves, and allspice) by ½ teaspoon.
- When substituting fruit juices in baking recipes, add ¼-½ teaspoon baking soda per cup of juice.

If you are interested in using wholegrain or transitional flour instead of bleached all-purpose flour, then I highly recommend a book by nutritionist Sara Sloan, which has an excellent section on working with these flours, as well as converting existing recipes to these ingredients. There are also some

good "not-too-sweet sweets" recipes. It's all in *The Brown Bag Cookbook*, available for $8.95 (add $2.00 for shipping) from Williamson Publishing in Charlotte, Vermont 05445.

WHAT ABOUT CHOCOLATE?

As every true chocolate lover knows, there's no adequate substitute for the real thing. However, if chocolate is off your diet, then try baking with carob chips when recipes call for semisweet chocolate pieces. Carob has a good taste all its own, and if you don't think of it as a chocolate substitute, you may surprise yourself and really like it.

Or you can go one step further, and substitute raisins, chopped dates, shredded coconut, chopped nuts, or chopped glazed fruits in recipes which include chocolate. In most of the bar cookie recipes in chapter 2 you can successfully work around the chocolate without sacrificing the cookie texture. They won't be chocolate cookies, but they'll still be good cookies!

BUTTER OR MARGARINE

This is an area that comes down to personal preference, dietary restraints, and cost efficiencies. If you use a particular brand of margarine for health reasons, then by all means you can bake with it, too. Some people (my daughter Elaine included) always bake with butter and feel it makes a much richer cookie that browns to that perfect honey color. Many good cooks recommend that you use at least one-third butter for your shortening, which is certainly one way to solve the dilemma. But I, personally, don't see a significant difference in overall results, and often choose margarine for my shortening. Six of one; half dozen of the other . . . you can decide for yourself.

I do, in some recipes, specifically recommend using a solid vegetable shortening, rather than butter or margarine. In these cases, follow my recommendation, and you'll have a much lighter textured cookie.

CUTTING COSTS WITH GENERIC BRANDS

Baking ingredients tend to be expensive. All those nuts, dried fruits, chocolate pieces and coconut flakes really add up, especially when you are doing a lot of baking for a big party or holiday.

Don't hesitate to buy the generic brands instead of the well-known name brands. Remember, you will be interested in a mingling of baked flavors, so you can use different standards than you might have for table foods or fresh ingredients. You'll find the generics work equally well for peanuts, chocolate pieces, powdered sugar, honey, peanut butter and jams. For example, the generic brand strawberry preserves has many fewer whole strawberries but still plenty of berry pieces which are all you need for baking.

SIFTING

If you use pre-sifted all-purpose flour, then you don't need to sift your flour before measuring. If flour is *not* pre-sifted, then sift once before measuring. In addition, I always sift the dry ingredients (flour, leavening, spices) together before adding them to the creamed butter, sugar, eggs, flavoring mixture. This guarantees a better mingling of flavors, a dispersement of all ingredients throughout the batter or dough, and therefore, a better batch of cookies.

If you have arthritis in your hands or your hands tire easily, then try using a fine sieve instead of a sifter. Simply press (actually, stir) the dry ingredients through the sieve with a wooden spoon. Works fine!

TO GREASE OR NOT TO GREASE

I tend to grease my cookie sheets for most of my recipes, because they are much easier to remove without breakage. However, greasing does encourage cookies to spread more. So for pressed cookies and cookie-cutter cookies, where shapes are more important, I usually don't grease the baking sheets.

You may find that using a non-stick pan works best for easy removal without breakage, as well as limited spreading. If you do choose to grease your pan, I recommend using a solid vegetable shortening.

As cookies cool, they get harder to remove from the pan, especially if it is ungreased. So remove them immediately to a wire rack for cooling. If for some reason they cool before you can remove them, pop them into a warm oven for a minute or two, and they should come off without breakage.

KNOW YOUR OVEN

Oven temperatures can vary as much as 50°, so get to know how your oven works, and then adjust baking times accordingly. I always set my timer a few minutes before the shortest baking time (if recipe says 18 to 20 minutes, I check in 15 minutes).

- Use the timer on your oven or purchase a small timer at the hardware store. It is so easy to forget those cookies in the oven, once you get involved in something else. So don't trust your memory – no matter how good it is.
- Remember, with cookies, even a few minutes can make a big difference, and overbaked cookies are always a disappointment.
- Be sure to preheat your oven so it will be ready when your batter is.

- Does your oven bake evenly or do the cookies in the back get done faster than those in the front? You may need to turn the pan halfway through baking time.
- Using a glass baking pan? Reduce oven temperature by 25°.

Always bake only one sheet at a time in the middle of your oven so the heat is evenly distributed. This is really very important. I think you'll be disappointed if you try to rush by putting two sheets in at once – not a good way to save time.

GETTING STARTED

Here are some general guidelines which may seem somewhat ritualistic, but actually are good baking habits to form.

Before You Start:
- Read through the complete recipe.
- Preheat your oven.
- Assemble all of your ingredients.
- Collect all of the necessary utensils.
- Grease pan.

Making the Batter:
- Always measure ingredients accurately for best results.
- Cream shortening, eggs, sugar, and flavoring together by hand or on medium speed with electric mixer. Add any liquid or melted chocolate.
- Sift flour if not pre-sifted; measure sifted flour.
- Next, sift the flour, leavening, and spices together, and then gradually add to the creamed mixture. Mix the batter together, until well-blended, and then beat by hand or with electric mixer on medium speed.

Baking:
- Spread batter evenly for bar cookies; for dropped cookies, strive for similar size to insure even baking of all cookies.
- Rotate cookie sheets so one is in oven; one is cooling; while the third one is being prepared.
- Set timer and check cookies sooner rather than later.
- Once baked, drop cookies should immediately be removed from baking sheet to cooling rack. Bar cookies can cool in the baking pan, which also should be placed on cooling rack to prevent overbaking.

One final tip: put ingredients away as you use each one. This way you'll avoid leaving something out or putting something in twice. Many a cookie batch has been saved by following this simple rule.

STORAGE

Be sure cookies have completely cooled before storing. Bar cookies are fine left in the baking pan, cut as needed, covered with foil.

Crisp drop, rolled, or shaped cookies do best when stored in a cookie jar or other container with a loose-fitting lid.

Soft cookies also do well in a cookie jar, but be sure the lid is tight-fitting. To keep them soft, place a piece of apple in the jar. Remember that cookies baked with honey tend to absorb more moisture.

FREEZING COOKIES: BAKE WHEN *YOU* WANT TO!

Almost all cookies freeze well if they are properly wrapped. I freeze mine in reuseable plastic containers and cookie tins. I always line my tins with waxed paper, and then put additional waxed paper between every layer of cookies, with a final sheet over the top cookie layer. This adequately prevents breakage and keeps cookies from sticking together.

Here are some other cookie freezing tips:
- Cool cookies completely before freezing.
- No tins or containers? Wrap in freezer paper (not waxed paper) which is moisture proof or use a coffee tin with tight-fitting lid.
- Pack only one kind of cookie in each tin or box. Never mix varieties because their flavors intermingle.
- Use air-tight containers with a good seal. Don't use cardboard boxes as the moisture seeps in.
- Avoid freezing cookies near strong-flavored foods, such as green peppers, garlic, etc. Somehow, even with careful wrapping, the cookies tend to pick up these flavors.
- Don't crowd cookies.
- Label containers carefully with cookie name, quantity, and date.
- For long-term freezing, wrap filled tins in freezer wrap.
- The shorter the time in the freezer the better the cookies, but they will stay relatively fresh if used in 3 to 4 months. After that, they begin to lose some of their flavor.
- Freeze refrigerator cookie dough, too. Simply wrap tightly in waxed paper, and then in freezer wrap. Refrigerator cookie dough should be frozen in 12″ × 2″ logs. To defrost, thaw at room temperature until dough can be handled.
- If you are going to freeze cookies which need powdered sugar sprinkled on them, wait and do this after you defrost them. This way they look absolutely fresh. The same is true for frosting cookies – wait until you are ready to use them.

Take advantage of the fact that cookies do freeze well. They make an instant homemade dessert whenever you need something special at the last minute.

DEFROSTING

It only take 10 to 15 minutes to defrost cookies. (If you have a microwave, cookies can be defrosted in 2 to 3 minutes on low.) Once defrosted, you can heat them briefly in a slow 300°F. oven to restore crispness.

MISCELLANEOUS TIPS AND REMINDERS

- Measure ingredients very carefully. Cookie-baking is precise in measurement.
- Measure dry ingredients in graduated measuring cups, leveling off with a knife.

Leveling off a Measuring Cup

- Measure liquids in a glass measuring cup, always with cup on a flat surface at eye level.
- Chill cookie dough well and keep tightly covered until you are ready to bake.
- Is your cookie dough sticky? You may have added too much liquid. Try adding a bit of flour.
- Cookie dough too dry? You may have too much flour so add some milk or cream, 1 teaspoon at a time.
- Cookies dry? Are they overbaked or did you add too much flour?
- Keep powdered sugar in a large metal salt shaker to sprinkle readily on cookies. Cinnamon works well this way, too.
- Be sure your baking sheet is completely cooled before dropping dough on it.

Sprinkling Cookies

- Cookies baked with molasses and brown sugar tend to burn easily, so check these more frequently.
- For brightly colored cookies, roll in colored sugar crystals while still warm.
- When adding food coloring to dough, remember a little goes a long, long way – 1 or 2 drops should be sufficient.
- To measure a half cup of peanut butter or solid shortening, fill glass measuring cup with half cup of water, add solid ingredient until water reaches full cup mark. Drain and remove with rubber spatula.
- Always crack eggs over a separate bowl so a spoiled egg or egg shell won't get into other ingredients.
- Never measure ingredients directly over the mixing bowl. To avoid accidentally spilling too much into the bowl, measure first over sink or counter, then add to other ingredients in mixing bowl.
- Baking in the morning? Assemble ingredients (I even measure the dry ingredients) and utensils the night before.

And remember, too, baking cookies is an enjoyable pastime, so be easy on yourself and spread the fun around by baking with a friend or child.

CHAPTER

2

Golde's Favorite Bar Cookies

Bar or pan cookies are so easy to prepare, that you'll wonder why you ever puchased the store-bought varieties. These are perfect for any impromptu gathering; many of these recipes are simple enough to whip up in your kitchen while you chat with some unexpected guests, and then serve them informally 30 minutes later. No mess, no fuss, and a warm gesture to let people know they're welcome in your home.

Bar cookies are also great for all those times when your kids are expected to bring a group snack to Brownie meetings or Little League practice, or a class party. Younger children can learn to bake some of the simple varieties like *Special Combination Cookies* or *Jam Squares* themselves. Best of all, you can cut the cookies to any size so there will always be enough if you suddenly have a bigger group than expected. In that sense, bar cookies are wonderfully versatile.

GOLDE'S BAR COOKIE BASICS

- Do grease your pan generously with vegetable shortening; be sure to cover bottom, corners and pan sides.
- Do use the specified size baking pan or very close it it.
- If you use a glass pan, reduce the oven temperature by 25°.
- Center the baking pan on the middle oven rack.
- Test to see if done 5 minutes before estimated time using same method you use for testing cakes (insert toothpick and see if it comes out clean).
- Cool thoroughly on wire rack before slicing.
- Cover pan tightly with foil to maintain freshness, as these cookies become stale quickly in open air.

- Experiment freely with these recipes using carob, coconut, dried fruit, chopped dates, raisins, nuts, ground cinnamon, ground nutmeg, preserves, grated zucchini, grated carrots, mincemeat, liqueurs for flavorings. Bar cookies are more versatile than most, and oftentimes if an experiment doesn't quite turn out, it can be resurrected as a great dessert, with a dollop of ice cream or whipped cream on top.

AVERAGE YIELDS

If you have an 8- or 9-inch-square baking pan, you can cut the squares as large as 2″ × 2″ (4 × 4 rows), yielding 16 squares, or as small as 2″ × 1″ (4 × 8 rows) yielding 32 squares. Anything much smaller is really too small, but you can see the versatility this creates.

If you have a larger baking pan, such as a 9″ × 13″ baking pan, the bars can be as large as 2⅛″ × 1½″ (6 × 6 rows) yielding 36 bars, or as small as 1⅝″ × 1½″ (8 × 6 rows) yielding 48 bars. Of course, these are approximate so don't get out your tape measure. Simply decide how many you need, and cut accordingly.

Seafoam Chews

A wonderfully sweet confection. A family favorite for many years!

Preparation time: 40 minutes
Pans: 15″ × 10″ jelly-roll pan or 9″ × 13″ baking pan, greased
Oven: 325°F. for 30 to 35 minutes
Yield: 54 small squares

Pastry:
½   cup soft butter or margarine
½   cup granulated sugar
½   cup brown sugar, packed
2   egg yolks (reserve whites)
1   teaspoon vanilla extract
2   cups all-purpose flour
2   teaspoons baking powder
1   teaspoon baking soda

½   teaspoon salt
3   tablespoons milk
1   cup (6 oz.) semisweet chocolate pieces

Topping:
2   egg whites
1   cup brown sugar, packed
¾   cup salted peanuts, coarsely chopped

Preheat oven to 325°F.

In a large bowl, cream together butter, granulated sugar and brown sugar. Beat in egg yolks and vanilla extract. Sift flour, baking powder, baking soda and salt together. Gradually add to creamed mixture and blend together. This gets quite thick, so add up to 3 tablespoons milk. Beat well into a fluffy light dough. Gently press dough into greased baking pan. Sprinkle chocolate pieces evenly over pastry and press down lightly.

In a medium bowl, beat the two egg whites until stiff. Gradually beat in the brown sugar. Spread this mixture evenly over the pastry layer. Top with chopped peanuts.

Bake for 30 to 35 minutes. Remove pan to wire rack to cool. Cut in squares when almost cool. These squares freeze very well.

Oriental Crunch

Delicious! Makes ordinary chocolate chip cookies seem bland and plain by comparison.

Preparation time: 15 to 20 minutes
Pan: 15" × 10" jelly-roll pan or 9" × 13" baking pan, greased lightly
Oven: 375°F. for 20 minutes
Yield: 48 squares

1 cup (2 sticks) butter, very soft	1 teaspoon vanilla extract
2 tablespoons instant coffee crystals	1 cup granulated sugar
2 tablespoons hot coffee	2 cups all-purpose flour
½ teaspoon salt	1 cup (6 oz.) semisweet chocolate pieces
½ teaspoon almond extract	1 cup almonds, broken or coarsely chopped

Preheat oven to 375°F.

Dissolve crystals in hot coffee. In a large bowl, cream together butter, coffee, salt, almond and vanilla extracts until smooth. Gradually add sugar, beating mixture until light and creamy. Blend in flour, then chocolate pieces and nuts. Press entire mixture lightly into a pan. (Don't press down too hard as the cookies should be crisp and light, not dense.) Bake for 20 minutes.

Cool pan on wire rack for about 5 minutes. Break cooled cookies into pieces like peanut brittle *or* while still warm, score into squares; then cool and break along the squars. Either way, these are wonderful and they freeze well, too! I promise this will be an oft' requested recipe.

Luscious Apricot Squares

These rich bars with plump apricots well-deserve to be described as "luscious." Served with your favorite hot beverage, these gems are sure to sweep away the pressures of the day.

Preparation time: 50 minutes   **Yield:** 32 bars
Pan: 8-inch-square pan, greased
Oven: 350°F. for 20–25 minutes (pastry)
        350°F. for 25–30 minutes (with topping)

Filling:
⅔   cup dried apricots
⅓   cup all-purpose flour, sifted
½   teaspoon baking powder
¼   teaspoon salt
1   cup brown sugar, packed
2   eggs, well beaten
½   teaspoon vanilla extract

½   cup walnuts, chopped
Powdered sugar
Pastry:
½   cup butter or margarine, softened
¼   cup granulated sugar
1   cup all-purpose flour, sifted

Preheat oven to 350°F.

Rinse apricots, cover with water, and boil 10 minutes. Drain and cool, then chop coarsely.

To make pastry, mix butter, granulated sugar and 1 cup flour until crumbly. Press pastry dough into pan. Bake for 20–25 minutes.

While pastry bakes, sift together ⅓ cup flour, baking powder, and salt. Set aside. In a large bowl, with mixer at low speed, gradually beat brown sugar into eggs. Add flour mixture, then vanilla. Stir in walnuts and apricots.

Spread apricot mixture evenly over baked layer. Bake for 25–30 minutes or until done. Cool in pan on wire rack. Cut into 32 bars and then roll or dip the bars in powdered sugar.

Winter Fruit Bars

Here's a versatile cookie that everyone likes. It makes a good mid-morning snack along with a glass of fruit juice.

Preparation time: 25 minutes
Pan: 2 cookie sheets, greased
Oven: 375°F. for 12–15 minutes
Yield: 40 cookies

¾ cup raisins	1 teaspoon vanilla extract
½ cup pitted dates, chopped	1 teaspoon cinnamon
2 tablespoons orange juice	¼ teaspoon nutmeg
½ cup butter or margarine, softened	1¾ cups flour
½ cup granulated sugar	½ teaspoon baking soda
½ cup brown sugar, packed	1 cup walnuts, coarsely chopped
2 eggs	½ teaspoon water

Preheat oven to 375°F.

In a small bowl, combine raisins, dates and orange juice. Set aside.

In a large bowl, combine butter, both sugars, 1 whole egg plus white from 1 additional egg, and vanilla. Set aside extra yolk. Beat butter mixture until light and fluffy. Add cinnamon, nutmeg, flour and baking soda and blend well. Stir in raisin mixture and walnuts.

Flour your hands and divide dough into 4 equal portions, 2 on each baking sheet. Shape into logs about 11″ long, 1½″ wide, and 1″ thick. Stir remaining egg yolk with water and brush top of logs.

Bake 12–15 minutes or until golden. Logs will feel soft but will become firm upon cooling. Remove pan to wire rack. Cool logs 10 minutes on pan. Slice diagonally into 1″ thick bars.

Cashew Caramel Yummies

The cashew-caramel combination is especially good if you leave the cashews in large chunks.

Preparation time: 20 minutes
Pan: 9-inch-square pan, greased
Oven: 350°F. for 20 minutes
Yield: 30 bars

Topping:

2 tablespoons butter or margarine, melted	½ teaspoon baking powder
1½ tablespoons light cream	¼ teaspoon salt
⅓ cup salted cashews, chunked	2 eggs, slightly beaten
¼ cup brown sugar	½ cup granulated sugar
Pastry:	½ cup brown sugar, packed
¾ cup all-purpose flour, sifted	½ cup salted cashews, coarsely chopped

Preheat oven to 350°F.

To prepare pastry, in a large bowl, mix the eggs and both sugars together. Blend in the nuts. Sift the flour with the baking powder and salt, and add to egg mixture, blending well. Bake for 20–25 minutes, until crust springs back to touch.

Meanwhile prepare topping in a medium bowl. Stir ¼ cup brown sugar, cream and cashews into the melted butter.

Spread evenly over baked pastry. Place under the broiler for about 1 minute or until topping bubbles and is golden brown. Cut into bars while cookies are warm. Cool in pan on wire rack.

Raspberry-Almond Meringue Squares

For the grown-up sweet tooth, these squares are sure to please.

Preparation time: 35 minutes   **Yield:** 35 squares
Pan: 9″ × 13″ baking pan lined with foil, grease foil
Oven: 350°F. for 25–30 minutes (pastry)
          350°F. for 20–25 minutes (topping)

Pastry:
1   cup butter or margarine, softened
7–8 oz. almond paste
½   cup light brown sugar, packed
1   large egg
½   teaspoon almond extract
2   cups all-purpose flour

Filling:
¾   cup red raspberry jam, seedless

Topping:
Whites from 3 large eggs
½   cup granulated sugar
½   cup coconut, flaked (optional)

Preheat oven to 350°F.

To prepare pastry, in a large bowl, beat butter, almond paste, and brown sugar until smooth. Beat in egg and almond extract. Stir in flour until well blended. Spread evenly in pan. Bake 25–30 minutes until golden. Cool slightly and spread with jam.

While pastry bakes, prepare topping. Beat egg whites until soft peaks form. Gradually beat in sugar until stiff peaks form.

Drop by tablespoonfuls over jam, and spread to cover. Sprinkle with coconut. Bake 20–25 minutes until topping is firm and golden. Remove pan to wire rack to cool completely. Lift foil out of pan, and cut into squares with sharp knife.

Dream Cake Bars

Coconut lovers really like this old-time recipe. I always like a cup of tea with Dream Cake Bars.

Preparation time: 20 minutes
Pan: 8-inch-square pan or 11" × 7" baking pan, ungreased
Oven: 350°F. for 10 minutes (pastry);
　　　350°F. for 25 to 30 minutes (with topping)
Yield: 25 bars

Pastry:
  1 cup all-purpose flour, sifted
  ¼ cup butter or margarine, softened
  2 tablespoons brown sugar

Topping:
  2 eggs
  1 cup brown sugar, packed
  ½ teaspoon baking powder
  3 tablespoons all-purpose flour
  1 teaspoon vanilla extract
  1 cup walnuts, coarsely chopped
  ¾ cup coconut, shredded

Preheat oven to 350°F.

In a medium bowl, mix pre-sifted flour, butter and 2 tablespoons brown sugar. Knead into light dough. Press gently into pan. Bake for 10 minutes.

Meanwhile, in a medium bowl, beat the two eggs lightly with a fork. Then add the remaining topping ingredients and mix thoroughly. Spread topping over partially baked pastry. Return pan to oven and bake an additional 25 to 30 minutes, until golden.

Cool completely on wire rack before cutting into squares. These freeze very well.

Light Lemon Squares

These are wonderfully light and tart. A favorite served with fresh fruit cup or sherbet.

Preparation time: 25 minutes
Pan: 8-inch-square pan, greased
Oven: 350°F. for 20 minutes (pastry);
       350°F. for 20 to 25 minutes (with topping)
Yield: 20 squares

Pastry:
1   cup all-purpose flour
½   cup (1 stick) butter or margarine
⅓   cup powdered sugar

Topping:
2   eggs
1   cup granulated sugar
½   tablespoon all-purpose flour
3   tablespoons lemon juice concentrate

Preheat oven to 350°F.

In a medium bowl, mix the pastry ingredients together. Press into a greased pan. Bake for 20 minutes.

Combine all topping ingredients together and beat until well-blended. Pour over baked pastry. Return to oven, and bake an additional 20 to 25 minutes.

Cool pan on wire rack before cutting. Sprinkle with additional sifted powdered sugar. These freeze quite well, although I think they taste fresher and lighter when freshly baked.

Chocolate Peanut Butter Fantasies

My grandchildren love these because they taste like chocolate peanut butter cups. These are so sweet, almost like a candy.

Preparation time: 35 minutes
Pan: 9″ × 13″ baking pan, ungreased

Oven: 350°F. for 12 minutes.
Yield: 36 squares

Pastry:

1½	cups all-purpose flour
⅔	cup brown sugar, firmly packed
½	teaspoon baking powder
¼	teaspoon salt
¼	teaspoon baking soda
⅔	cup butter or margarine, softened
2	egg yolks, beaten
½	teaspoon vanilla extract

Topping:

1¼	cups powdered sugar
¾	cup unsalted peanuts, finely chopped
¼	cup butter or margarine, melted
1½	cups peanut butter
½	teaspoon vanilla extract
1	(12 oz.) package semisweet chocolate pieces

Preheat oven to 350°F.

Combine all the pastry ingredients together in a large bowl, and beat at low speed until it is a crumbly consistency. Press crumbs into an ungreased baking pan. Bake for 12 minutes or until golden brown.

Set aside chocolate pieces. In medium bowl, mix remaining topping ingredients together and set aside.

Turn off the oven and remove baked pastry. Let it cool for about 2 minutes, and while still warm spread the topping evenly over the pastry. Sprinkle chocolate pieces over the topping and return to warm oven for 2 to 3 minutes until chocolate has softened enough to spread. Remove from oven and spread chocolate evenly, like a frosting. Cool before cutting.

Merlene's Hermits

These can be baked as a bar cookie or they can be formed into a drop cookie. Either way, they are rich, chewy, and spicy just like Hermits should be!

Preparation time: 20 minutes
Pan: 1 cookie sheet, greased
Oven: 325°F. for 25 minutes
Yield: 48 bars

1 cup butter or margarine, softened	3¼ cups all-purpose flour
1½ cups granulated sugar	1 teaspoon baking soda
1 teaspoon ground allspice	½ teaspoon salt
1 teaspoon ground cinnamon	½ cup molasses
1 teaspoon ground cloves	1 cup seedless raisins
3 eggs	½ cup nuts, chopped (optional)

Preheat oven to 325°F.

In large bowl, cream together the butter, sugar and spices. Add eggs, one at a time, blending them into the creamed mixture. Then add all remaining ingredients, and mix thoroughly. Spread cookie batter on greased cookie sheet. Bake for 25 minutes. Cut into bars while still warm, and cool cookies on wire rack. Makes 48 bars which freeze beautifully.

Variation: If you prefer drop cookies, preheat oven to 375°F. Drop batter by rounded teaspoonfuls onto greased cookie sheet. Bake for 12 to 15 minutes; check often so these don't burn around the edges. Cool cookies on wire rack.

Special Combination Cookies

These are so easy that the kids love making them; so delicious that everyone loves eating them.

Preparation time: 10 minutes
Pan: 9″ × 13″ baking pan, ungreased
Oven: 375°F. for 20 to 30 minutes
Yield: 48 squares

½ cup (1 stick) butter or margarine	1 (12 oz.) package semisweet chocolate pieces
1 cup graham cracker crumbs	1 can sweetened condensed milk
1 cup flaked coconut	½ cup chopped nuts (walnuts, peanuts or pecans)

Preheat oven to 375°F.

Melt butter in baking pan. Add remaining ingredients to baking pan, one at a time, in layers – i.e., first a layer of all the graham cracker crumbs, then a layer of all of the coconut, until all ingredients have been layered. Do not stir. Bake for 25 to 30 minutes. Cool pan on wire rack. Cut in squares. These are never quite as good after being frozen, but they are so quick and easy, that there really is no need to make them in advance.

Variations: Substitute 16 ounces glazed fruit for chocolate pieces, or 12 ounces of raisins, dates, and prunes (chopped).

Pecan Pie Treasures

A pecan pie lovers dream come true! These taste as good as pecan pie with much less effort. Wonderful served with whipped cream or ice cream on top.

Preparation time: 25 minutes
Pan: 9-inch-square baking pan, greased
Oven: 350°F. for 15 minutes (pastry);
350°F. for 25 to 30 minutes (topping)
Yield: 32 bars

Pastry:

1   cup all-purpose flour
½   cup quick rolled oats, uncooked
½   cup butter or margarine, softened
¾   cup brown sugar, firmly packed

Topping:

1   tablespoon all-purpose flour
3   eggs
¾   cup dark corn syrup
¾   cup pecans, coarsely chopped
½   teaspoon vanilla extract
Dash of salt

Preheat oven to 350°F.

In medium bowl, combine all pastry ingredients. Mix together until a crumbly mixture is formed. Press into greased baking pan. Bake 15 minutes.

Meanwhile, combine the topping ingredients, mixing thoroughly. Pour over baked pastry, and bake for an additional 25 to 30 minutes, until golden brown.

Cool pan on wire rack before cutting into bars. These freeze perfectly, and are wonderful to have on hand for a quick dessert. Try topping with coffee ice cream, or whipped cream flavored with Grand Marnier.

Toffee Bars

Not-too-sweet with lots of crunch, this versatile bar cookie has special appeal when served with a steaming mug of fresh-brewed coffee.

Preparation time: 20 minutes
Pan: 9" × 13" baking pan, greased
Oven: 375°F. for 15 minutes
Yield: 48 small bars

Pastry:
½ cup butter or margarine, softened
½ cup light brown sugar, firmly packed
1 egg yolk
1 teaspoon vanilla extract
½ cup all-purpose flour, sifted
½ cup quick rolled oats, uncooked

Topping:
3 squares semisweet chocolate
1 tablespoon butter or margarine
½ cup walnuts or pecans, coarsely chopped

Preheat oven to 375°F.

In a large bowl, cream butter, sugar, vanilla extract, and egg yolk until smooth. Add the sifted flour and rolled oats. Stir until well-blended.

Press dough into pan. Bake 15 minutes or until golden. Remove from oven; cool slightly.

Meanwhile, melt chocolate and butter in a double boiler over hot, but not boiling water. Spread chocolate mixture over warm baked pastry. Sprinkle with nuts.

Score into bars while still warm. Cool completely before removing from pan.

Apricot Squares

These squares are so easy to make, yet so lovely, light, and elegant. Just right served with tea in your favorite china cups.

Preparation time: 10 minutes
Pan: 15″ × 10″ jelly-roll pan or 9″ × 13″ baking pan, greased
Oven: 350°F. for 30 minutes
Yield: 32 squares

Pastry:
2   cups all-purpose flour
1   cup (2 sticks) butter or margarine, softened
2   egg yolks

1   teaspoon vanilla extract
¾   cup brown sugar, packed

Topping:
10   oz. jar apricot preserves
½   cup nuts, coarsely chopped

Preheat oven to 350°F.

In a medium bowl, combine all pastry ingredients and mix thoroughly until light dough forms. Press into greased pan. Spread apricot preserves evenly over pastry. Sprinkle chopped nuts on top.

Bake for 30 minutes. Remove from oven; score into squares but leave in baking pan. Return pan to oven with heat turned off for 15 minutes more. Complete cooling on rack.

Apricot Squares don't freeze well, as they tend to break, but they are so easy to prepare that you'll find yourself baking them quite often.

Variations: You can substitute any kind of preserves (the thicker the better); I often use ginger-marmalade. I usually use chopped walnuts, but again, use what you most enjoy. If you are a coconut fan, then sprinkle some on instead of the nuts.

Honey Zucchini-Nut Bars

Chewy, nutty, and extra moist, these are as good as they sound.
A nice way to use extra large zucchinis, too.

Preparation time: 20 minutes
Pan: 9″ × 13″ baking pan, greased
Oven: 350°F. for 25 to 30 minutes
Yield: 40 bars

Pastry:
¼ cup butter, melted
1 cup honey
3 eggs, well-beaten
1¼ cups all-purpose flour
1 teaspoon baking powder
¾ cup shredded zucchini,
    squeezed dry

1 cup dates, finely chopped
1 cup walnuts, chopped
Dash of salt

Topping:
⅓ cup sifted powdered sugar

Preheat oven to 350°F.

Mix pastry ingredients together in order listed. Spread into greased baking pan. Bake for 25 to 30 minutes, until lightly brown. Cut into finger-sized pieces. While still warm, roll in sifted powdered sugar. These freeze well, but roll in powdered sugar *after* removing from freezer.

Variation: This recipe is good with 1 cup sunflower nutmeats instead of walnuts.

Golde's Best Brownies

I have to admit – these are so good that you'll never settle for anything less again. It's a brownie worth raving about!

Preparation time: 30 minutes
Pan: 9″ × 13″ baking pan, greased
Oven: 350°F. for 25 minutes
Yield: 60 brownies

1 cup vegetable shortening	1½ teaspoons salt
4 squares semisweet chocolate	2 teaspoons vanilla
4 eggs, beaten slightly	1 cup nuts, chopped (optional)
2 cups granulated sugar	3 tablespoons light corn syrup
1½ cups all-purpose flour	
1 teaspoon baking powder	

Preheat oven to 350°F.

In the top of a double boiler, melt the shortening and chocolate, watching carefully to avoid scorching. Pour into a large bowl. (Be sure to use a rubber spatula to get all the chocolate out of the saucepan.) Add the lightly beaten eggs, and then gradually add the sugar, mixing thoroughly.

Sift together the flour, baking powder and salt. Add to the chocolate mixture and blend well. Lastly, mix in the vanilla, nuts and syrup.

Pour batter into greased pan and bake for 25 minutes. Cool pan on wire rack. Cut into squares when cool. These freeze perfectly, and are still delicious as long as 6 months later.

Everyone's Favorite Cream Cheese Brownies

As popular as cream cheese brownies have become, this is still my old favorite recipe.

Preparation time: 30 minutes
Pan: 8- or 9-inch square baking pan, greased
Oven: 350°F. for 35 to 40 minutes
Yield: 24 brownies

Chocolate batter:

4   ounces German's sweet chocolate
3   tablespoons butter or margarine
2   eggs, beaten
¾   cup granulated sugar
½   teaspoon baking powder
¼   teaspoon salt
½   cup all-purpose flour
½   cup nuts, chopped

1   teaspoon vanilla extract

Cheese batter:

2   tablespoons butter
1   (3 oz.) package cream cheese
¼   cup granulated sugar
1   egg
1   tablespoon all-purpose flour
½   teaspoon vanilla extract

Preheat oven to 350°F.

In a double boiler, melt the chocolate with 3 tablespoons butter, stirring constantly. Set aside to cool.

Meanwhile, in medium bowl, beat 2 eggs until thick and lemon colored. Gradually add ¾ cup granulated sugar, beating until thickened. Add baking powder, salt and ½ cup flour. Once chocolate is cool, blend it in along with the nuts, and 1 teaspoon vanilla extract. Set aside.

In small bowl, cream 2 tablespoons butter with the cream cheese. Gradually add ¼ cup sugar. Cream well after each additional ingredient. Blend in 1 egg, 1 tablespoon flour, ½ teaspoon vanilla extract.

Spread about half of the chocolate batter in a greased 8- or 9-inch baking pan. Then layer on all of the cheese batter. Spoon on the remaining chocolate batter in various spots. Zigzag through the batter with a rubber spatula in order to create a marbling effect.

Bake for 35 to 40 minutes. Cool on wire rack before cutting into squares.

This freezes beautifully as long as you are sure to put waxed paper between layers.

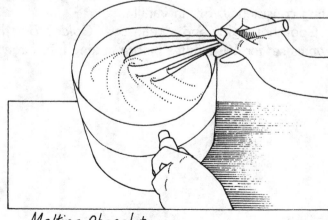

Melting Chocolate

Double-Fudge Brownies Supreme

Prepare Golde's Best Brownies, but do not cut into squares. Frost with this topping and you'll have a wonderfully rich (but not too sweet) chocolate dessert.

Frosting preparation time: 15 minutes

2	squares semisweet chocolate	½	cup granulated sugar
		1	tablespoon cornstarch
1	tablespoon butter or margarine	¾	cup milk
		½	teaspoon vanilla extract

In a heavy saucepan, melt the butter and chocolate together being careful not to scorch the mixture. Add sugar and cornstarch and blend thoroughly. Add milk and continue cooking, stirring constantly, until thick frosting consistency. Stir in vanilla.

Cool thoroughly and spread over *Golde's Best Brownies*. Let frosted brownies set for 10 minutes before cutting into large cake-like squares.

Mocha Java Dessert Bars

This chocolate-lovers cookie is a complete dessert in itself. If you really want to treat yourself royally, use a fine Dutch cocoa and gourmet-quality white chocolate.

Preparation time: 40 minutes
Pan: 9-inch-square baking pan, greased
Oven: No baking required
Yield: 15 dessert bars or 30 smaller bars

Filling:
2 teaspoons instant coffee crystals
2 tablespoons hot coffee
2½ cups powdered sugar
¼ cup cocoa
¼ cup butter or margarine, softened
2 tablespoons milk

Topping:
6 oz. white chocolate bar

Pastry:
½ cup butter or margarine
½ cup granulated sugar
1 teaspoon vanilla extract
1 egg, slightly beaten
2 cups graham cracker crumbs
½ cup nuts, finely chopped
¾ cup coconut

To prepare pastry, combine ½ cup butter, sugar, vanilla and egg in a double boiler. Stir constantly until slightly thickened. Add graham cracker crumbs, coconut, and nuts. Mix well. Spread evenly in baking pan. Let stand 15 minutes.

Meanwhile, prepare filling. In medium-sized bowl, dissolve instant coffee in hot coffee. Blend in powdered sugar, cocoa, ¼ cup butter and milk. Spread filling over pastry and chill for 15 minutes.

To prepare topping, melt white chocolate in microwave or over double boiler. Cool slightly. Spread over filling. Cut into squares. Refrigerate.

Spiced Carrot Squares

No eggs are used in this cookie recipe which is as good as carrot cake, if not better! It's a wonderful treat for all those who are restricting their cholesterol.

Preparation time: 30 minutes
Pan: 9″ × 13″, greased
Oven: 325°F. for 35–40 minutes
Yield: 24 squares

¾ cup granulated sugar
1   cup grated carrot
1   cup raisins
1   teaspoon cinnamon
1   teaspoon nutmeg
1   teaspoon ground cloves
1½ cups water or 1 cup water plus ½ cup orange juice

3   tablespoons margarine
2   cups flour
2   teaspoons baking soda
¼   teaspoon salt
1   cup walnuts, coarsely chopped

Preheat oven to 325°F.

In a small saucepan, combine water, sugar, carrots, raisins, and spices. Bring mixture to a boil. Reduce heat and simmer for 5 minutes.

Pour mixture into large mixing bowl, and cool to lukewarm.

Add flour, baking soda, and salt. Mix well. Stir in walnuts. Bake for 35–40 minutes or until tester comes out clean. Cool pan on wire rack before cutting into squares.

Lemony Pecan Bars

The lemon and pecan flavors meld so well together. These will become a favorite, especially for summertime picnics and barbecues.

Preparation time: 30 minutes
Pan: 9″ × 13″ baking pan, greased
Oven: 325°F. for 15 minutes (pastry);
　　　325°F. for 35 to 40 minutes with topping
Yield: 30 bars

Pastry:
½　cup butter or margarine, softened
2　cups all-purpose flour, sifted
½　cup powdered sugar

Topping:
4　eggs, slightly beaten
1½　cups granulated sugar
½　cup lemon juice concentrate
½　teaspoon baking powder
1　cup pecans, coarsely chopped

Preheat oven to 325°F.

In a large bowl, cream together all the pastry ingredients until well-blended. Press the mixture evenly into a greased baking pan. Bake for 15 minutes.

Meanwhile, combine all topping ingredients. Stir well. Pour over the baked pastry. Return to oven and bake an additional 35 to 40 minutes or until golden brown. Cool pan on wire rack. Sprinkle with sifted powdered sugar if desired. Cut into bars when cool.

Oatmeal Date Bars

Rich with brown sugar, these are popular with oatmeal cookie lovers.
They go perfectly with a glass of cold milk, too!

Preparation time: 40 minutes
Pan: 9″ × 13″ baking pan, greased
Oven: 400°F. for 20 to 25 minutes
Yield: 48 bars

Filling:
2   (8 oz.) packages dates, chopped
⅔   cup water
¾   cup granulated sugar
2   tablespoons lemon juice concentrate

Pastry:
1½   cups flour, sifted
1   cup brown sugar, packed
1½   cups quick-cooking rolled oats, uncooked
½   teaspoon salt
¾   cup vegetable shortening

Preheat oven to 400°F.

In a heavy sauce pan, combine all filling ingredients and cook about 8 minutes or until thick. Set aside to cool.

Sift flour before measuring. In a large bowl, combine flour, brown sugar, oats and salt. Cut in the shortening until coarse crumbs form.

Press half of pastry in the pan. Cover the pastry with all of the filling. Spread remaining pastry over the top.

Bake for 20 to 25 minutes until golden. Remove to wire rack. Cool before cutting into squares. These freeze very well.

Coffee-Pecan Chewies

The hint of coffee combined with pecans produces a provocative confection.

Preparation time: 35 minutes
Pan: 8-inch-square pan, greased
Oven: 350°F. for 35 minutes
Yield: 24 bars

¾ cup all-purpose flour	¼ cup butter, melted
1 teaspoon powdered instant coffee	1 teaspoon vanilla extract
½ teaspoon salt	½ cup pecans, coarsely chopped
2 eggs	⅓ cup sifted powdered sugar
1 cup sugar	

Preheat oven to 350°F.

Sift flour, coffee and salt. Set aside.

In a large bowl, beat eggs until foamy. Add sugar and continue beating until quite thick. Stir in melted butter and vanilla extract.

Add dry sifted ingredients and mix well. Fold in nuts.

Bake for 35 minutes until golden brown. Remove pan to wire rack. Cool before cutting. Sprinkle with powdered sugar if desired.

These freeze very well.

Fruit Squares

Quick and easy, yet oh-so-good. This recipe is ideal when baking with young children — just enough mixing, patting, spreading and decorating to keep them interested (and make them very proud when they're done).

Preparation time: 10 minutes
Pan: 9″ × 13″ baking pan, greased
Oven: 350°F. for 18 to 20 minutes
Yield: 48 squares

Pastry:
¾ cup butter or margarine
⅓ cup powdered sugar
1½ cups all-purpose flour

Topping:
10 ounce jar of favorite jam or preserve
1 cup coconut flakes (optional)
1 cup chopped nuts (optional)

Preheat oven to 350°F.

In a medium bowl, blend the pastry ingredients together. Press dough into a 9″ × 13″ greased pan. Spread your favorite preserves evenly over pastry. Sprinkle with flaked coconut or chopped nuts.

Bake for 18 to 20 minutes. For best results, refrigerate for several hours before cutting into squares.

Variation 1: I use apricot, peach, raspberry or strawberry preserves. You may want to mix two kinds together. Or you may want to bake half a panful in one flavor, the other half pan in another flavor for both color and flavor contrasts.

Variation 2: For added flavor and a bit of tang to offset the sweetness, grate about 1 tablespoon orange or lemon peel into the preserves before spreading.

Variation 3: If you prefer sprinkling with chopped nuts instead of coconut before baking, try using sunflower nutmeats. Shake some powdered sugar on when you remove the pan from the oven, while squares are still hot.

Grating citrus peels

Applesauce n'Fudge Bars

The applesauce keeps these moist and fresh. The chocolate gives them a fudgy richness.

Preparation time: 20 minutes
Pan: 8- or 9-inch-square pan, greased
Oven: 350°F. for 30 minutes
Yield: 24 bars

2   squares unsweetened chocolate
½   cup (1 stick) butter or margarine
⅔   cup sweetened applesauce
2   eggs, beaten
1   cup brown sugar, firmly packed

1   teaspoon vanilla extract
1   cup all-purpose flour, sifted
½   teaspoon baking powder
¼   teaspoon baking soda
¼   teaspoon salt
½   cup walnuts, chopped

Preheat oven to 350°F.

Melt chocolate and butter together. Set aside.

In a large bowl, mix applesauce, eggs, sugar, and vanilla extract together. Sift the dry ingredients together. Gradually mix into the applesauce mixture. Blend well. Add melted chocolate and stir well.

Pour into greased pan. Sprinkle with chopped walnuts. Bake for 30 minutes. Remove pan to rack and cool. Cut into bars.

These freeze well, and stay fresh (if well-covered) for an unusually long time.

Chocolate Chip Cookie Bars

A favorite with kids of all ages and so easy to make.

Preparation time: 20 to 25 minutes
Pan: 15″ × 10″ jelly-roll pan, ungreased
Oven: 350°F. for 20 minutes
Yield: 48 bars

1	cup butter or margarine, very soft	Dash salt	
1	cup light brown sugar, packed	1	cup (6 oz.) semisweet chocolate pieces
1	teaspoon vanilla extract	¾	cup pecans or walnuts, coarsely chopped
2	cups flour		

Preheat oven to 350°F.

In a large bowl, beat the butter and sugar until fluffy. Add the vanilla extract. Sift the salt plus flour into the butter mixture and blend well. Fold in chocolate pieces and nuts.

Press batter into an ungreased jelly-roll pan. Bake for 20 minutes until golden brown. While warm score into bars and cool in pan on wire rack.

These freeze very well if they last that long!

Heavenly Chocolate Nut Meltaways

Ahhh . . . and what a heavenly treat these are! A surprise chocolate layer wrapped in a light pastry with a rich, nutty topping.

Preparation time: 40 minutes
Pan: 9″ × 13″ baking pan, greased
Oven: 350°F. for 10 minutes (pastry);
       350°F. for 30 to 35 minutes (topping)
Yield: 48 squares

Pastry:
½   cup (1 stick) butter or margarine
1   egg yolk
2   tablespoons water
1½ cups all-purpose flour
1   teaspoon granulated sugar
1   teaspoon baking powder
1   cup (6 oz.) semisweet chocolate pieces

Topping:
2   eggs
¾   cups granulated sugar
6   tablespoons butter or margarine, melted
2   teaspoons vanilla extract
2   cups nuts, coarsely chopped

Preheat oven to 350°F.

To make pastry, in a medium bowl, beat together the ½ cup butter, egg yolk, and water. Stir in the flour, 1 teaspoon sugar and baking powder. Mix together. Pat into a greased 9″ × 13″ pan. Bake for 10 minutes.

Remove from oven, and sprinkle with chocolate pieces. Return to oven for 1 minute to melt. Remove from oven and spread chocolate as you would a frosting. Set aside.

To make the topping, in a small bowl, beat the 2 eggs and ¾ cup sugar together. Stir in the melted butter and vanilla extract. When well-blended, fold in the chopped nuts. Spread topping over chocolate layer. Bake in 350° oven for 30 to 35 minutes. Remove to wire rack to cool. Cut into squares while still warm, but leave in pan until ready to use or freeze.

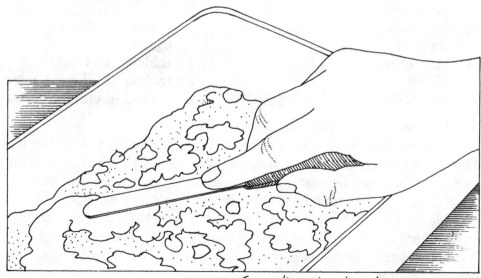

Spreading the Chocolate Pieces

Creamy Cheesecake Bars

As rich and creamy as the best cheesecake, and much easier to bake.
This recipe is a longtime staple of mine, still the best one of its kind.

Preparation time: 25 minutes
Pan: 8-inch-square pan, ungreased
Oven: 350°F. for 12 to 15 minutes (pastry);
   350°F. for 25 to 30 minutes (filling)
Yield: 36 bars

Pastry:
⅓   cup butter or margarine, softened
⅓   cup brown sugar, firmly packed
1   cup all-purpose flour, sifted
⅓   cup walnuts, finely chopped

Filling:
¼   cup granulated sugar
1   (8 oz.) package cream cheese, softened
1   egg, beaten
2   tablespoons milk
1   tablespoon lemon juice
½   teaspoon vanilla extract

Preheat oven to 350°F.

In a medium bowl, cream the butter and brown sugar together until light. Add the sifted flour and chopped walnuts. Mix until crumbs form. Set aside 2 cups to use as topping. Press remaining crumb mixture into ungreased pan. Bake for 12 to 15 minutes. Cool pan on rack.

Meanwhile, in a small bowl, beat the granulated sugar and cream cheese until smooth. Add remaining ingredients and beat thoroughly.

Spread this mixture over the baked crumb crust. Sprinkle reserved crumbs as a topping.

Bake for 25 to 30 minutes. Remove pan to rack to cool. Cut in bars and refrigerate as these will spoil if left unrefrigerated. Garnish each square with a half of a strawberry if you like. These freeze very well.

Date-Nut Squares

If you like the chewiness of dates, you'll love these. A perfect cookie for brunch or tea on a brisk autumn day.

Preparation time: 30 minutes
Pan: 9″ × 13″ baking pan, greased
Oven: 350°F. for 20 to 25 minutes
Yield: 60 small squares

¾ cup all-purpose flour	1 cup granulated sugar
¼ teaspoon baking powder	2 eggs, beaten
⅛ teaspoon salt (optional)	1 cup walnuts, chopped fine
½ cup butter or margarine, melted	1 cup dates, cut fine
	½ cup powdered sugar

Preheat oven to 350°F.

Sift flour, baking powder and salt together; set aside.

In a medium bowl, mix together melted butter, sugar and beaten eggs. When well-blended, gradually add sifted dry ingredients. Mix well and fold in nuts and dates.

Spread dough on greased baking pan, and bake for 20 to 25 minutes. Remove pan to wire rack and cut in bars while still warm. Roll warm squares in powdered sugar.

To freeze: Freeze squares before rolling in powdered sugar. After defrosting, warm squares in 300°F. oven for 3 to 5 minutes, and then proceed to roll in powdered sugar. Cookies will look much fresher this way!

Butter Pecan Turtle Bars

The brown sugar gives these a rich color, and a very rich flavor.

Preparation time: 35 to 40 minutes
Pan: 9″ × 13″ baking pan, ungreased
Oven: 350°F. for 18 to 20 minutes
Yield: 42 bars

Pastry:
2   cups all-purpose flour
1   cup brown sugar, firmly packed
½   cup sweet butter, softened
1-1½ cups pecan halves

Topping:
⅔   cup sweet butter
½   cup brown sugar, firmly packed
1   cup (6 oz.) semisweet chocolate pieces

Preheat oven to 350°F.

In a medium bowl, blend flour, 1 cup brown sugar and ½ cup softened sweet butter on medium speed (or by hand with a fork) until mixture is in fine particles. Press firmly into ungreased 9″ × 13″ baking pan. Sprinkle pecans evenly over unbaked pastry.

In heavy saucepan, combine ⅔ cup sweet butter and ½ cup brown sugar. Cook over medium heat, stirring constantly, until entire surface begins to boil. Continue boiling for 1 minute while still stirring. Pour mixture over the pastry.

Bake for 18 to 20 minutes or until topping layer is bubbly and pastry is golden brown.

Remove pan from oven to wire rack and sprinkle with chocolate pieces. Do not spread. Allow chocolate pieces to melt slightly and then swirl as they melt. Leave some chocolate pieces whole.

Cool and cut into bars. These freeze well. A wonderful treat!

Spicy Applesauce-Raisin Squares

Bake these in the fall when you're making homemade applesauce. They'll fill your kitchen with a spicy aroma, and you'll know that autumn is here.

Preparation time: 35 minutes
Pan: 15″ × 10″ jelly-roll pan or 9″ × 13″ baking pan, greased
Oven: 350°F. for 25 minutes
Yield: 36 squares

2 cups all-purpose flour, sifted	1 egg
2 teaspoons baking soda	1 teaspoon vanilla extract
¾ teaspoon ground cinnamon	1½ cups applesauce
¼ teaspoon ground cloves	¾ cup walnuts or pecans, chopped
¼ teaspoon ground nutmeg	¾ cup light or dark seedless raisins
½ cup (1 stick) butter or margarine, softened	Powdered sugar
1 cup granulated sugar	

Preheat oven to 350°F.

Sift pre-sifted flour, baking soda, and three spices together. Set aside.

In a large bowl, cream butter and sugar together until fluffy. Add the egg and vanilla extract and beat well. Add the sifted flour mixture, and mix just enough to combine. Add applesauce, nuts and raisins. Stir with spoon until well-blended.

Bake for 20 to 25 minutes. Remove pan to wire rack to cool.

Sprinkle with sifted powdered sugar, and cut into squares. Or, these can be cut into large cake-like squares and served with a dollop of homemade whipped cream.

Lemony Coconut Delights

These two flavors belong together. Here they're made even richer by the brown sugar filling.

Preparation time: 35 minutes
Pan: 9″ × 13″ baking pan, greased
Oven: 325°F. for 10 to 15 minutes (pastry);
     350°F. for 20 minutes (filling)
Yield: 48 squares

Pastry:
1½ cups all-purpose flour, sifted
½   cup brown sugar, firmly packed
½   cup butter or margarine, softened

Topping:
1   cup powdered sugar
1   tablespoon butter or margarine, melted
½   teaspoon grated lemon rind
Juice of 1 lemon

Filling:
2   eggs, beaten
1   cup brown sugar, firmly packed
1   cup flaked coconut
1   cup nuts, chopped
2   tablespoons all-purpose flour
½   teaspoon baking powder
¼   teaspoon salt
¼   teaspoon vanilla extract

Preheat oven to 325°F.

In a medium bowl, mix together pastry ingredients until a dough forms. Press the dough into a greased baking pan. Bake for 10 to 15 minutes. Remove from oven. Reset oven to 350°.

In the meantime, combine all the filling ingredients in a small bowl. Mix until well-blended. Spread over pastry and bake for 20 minutes at 350°F.

Mix topping ingredients together. While cookies are still warm, spread topping over baked pastry. Cool slightly and cut into squares.

Graham Pecan Wafers

Very sweet, very good, very easy.

Preparation time: 10 minutes
Pan: 15″ × 10″ jelly-roll pan, lined with foil
Oven: 350°F. for 15 minutes
Yield: 70 cookies

16 whole graham crackers (or enough to cover bottom of your pan)
1 cup (2 sticks) butter or margarine
1 cup brown sugar
1 cup (heaping) pecans, chopped

Preheat oven to 350°F.

Place graham crackers side by side on lined pan.

Bring butter and brown sugar to a boil. Be careful not to scorch. When mixture bubbles, add pecans. Mix well and pour over graham crackers, spreading evenly to cover.

Bake for 15 minutes. Remove from oven and cut each wafer in half. When cool, break in half again to make strips.

3

Golde's Best Drop Cookies

Drop cookies demand a bit more time and attention, but they are still easy to prepare and are well worth any extra effort. There is nothing quite like the look of a smiling face crunching into a *Chocolate Chip Crisper* or a cinnamon *Snickerdoodle*. And drop cookies, after all, are what we think of when we think of "cookies," or cookie jar, or even Cookie Monster!

Here are a few do's and don'ts to help you have success with every batch you bake.

- Spoon by the rounded or heaping (for larger cookies) teaspoonful, using a regular flatware teaspoon rather than a measuring teaspoon. Use a rubber spatula to push batter onto cookie sheet.
- Strive for general uniformity in size and shape; this way all your cookies will be done at approximately the same time.
- Leave adequate space between teaspoonfuls of cookie batter; remember these cookies spread as they bake. I usually leave about 2 inches between medium-sized cookies.
- Be sure to grease cookie sheets adequately, unless otherwise directed. I recommend using vegetable shortening for this. If your cookies spread too much, then cut down on greasing or use a non-stick pan. If you don't use grease, be sure to remove cookies from the sheet while still hot.
- Keep close watch on cookies while they bake until you really get to know your oven and your cookie sheet. Drop cookies bake very quickly and are apt to burn around the edges or on the bottom if not closely tended.
- Remove cookies from the cookie sheets as soon as possible to stop the baking process. Cool cookies on wire racks (raised slightly above counter) for best results.

- Drop cookies are perfect for double-batching. Consider always doubling your recipe – some for now and some all baked and popped into the freezer.
- Giant-sized cookies are popular now. Just use more batter and, of course, adjust space between each to allow for spreading. Kids love these, plus they're great fun at picnics. Try *Chocolate Chip Crispers, Crispy Oatmeal-Raisin Cookies,* and *Spicy Fruit Cookies* (all in chapter 3) for giants.
- Drop cookies aren't as versatile as bar cookies when it comes to altering recipes. You can feel fairly confident about interchanging kinds of nuts, sunflower seed meats, raisins, chopped dates, chopped apricots, carob bits, chocolate pieces, butterscotch pieces, flavored extracts, and flaked coconut, but keep the basic batter as recommended in each recipe.

Putting Batter onto Cookie Sheet

Chocolate Meringue Fluffs

Chocolate fanciers will love these chocolaty, chewy meringues. Be sure to double your batch because these go as fast as you can refill the platter!

Preparation time: 30 minutes
Pan: cookie sheets, greased
Oven: 350°F. for 10 minutes
Yield: 80 cookies

1 cup (6 oz.) semisweet chocolate pieces	⅓ cup graham cracker crumbs
3 egg whites	½ teaspoon vanilla extract
1 cup granulated sugar	

Preheat oven to 350°F.

In a double boiler or microwave, melt the chocolate pieces. Let chocolate cool for 5 minutes.

Meanwhile, in a medium bowl beat egg whites until stiff, but not too dry. Gradually add the sugar and beat until smooth and glossy. Fold in, with a wooden spoon, the melted chocolate, the graham cracker crumbs and the vanilla extract.

Drop by level teaspoonfuls onto greased cookie sheet. Bake for 10 minutes. Cool cookies on baking sheet for 2 to 3 minutes for easier removal.

Chocolate Meringue Fluffs freeze fairly well, though they tend to lose some of their fluffy texture once frozen, and they break easily. So I'd suggest you freeze some other kind, and save these quick and easy meringues for immediate use.

Lemon Macadamia Cookies

Refreshingly different – perfect for a summer's day with tall frosted glasses of iced tea.

Preparation time: 40 minutes
Pan: baking sheets, greased
Oven: 375°F., 7–9 minutes
Yield: 60 cookies

1½ cups macadamia nuts, coarsely chopped	¼ teaspoon baking powder
2 eggs	3 teaspoons grated lemon peel
1⅓ cups light brown sugar, packed	2 teaspoons fresh lemon juice
½ cup plus 1 tablespoon flour	Pinch of salt

Preheat oven to 375°F.

Spread nuts on baking sheet, and bake until lightly browned, about 8–10 minutes. Cool.

In a large bowl, beat eggs on high speed, until light and fluffy (about 3 minutes). Gradually add sugar and continue to beat until well blended. Sift together baking powder and flour. Add flour mixture, lemon peel, lemon juice, salt, and nuts to sugar mixture. Blend well.

Drop by rounded teaspoonfuls about 3″ apart on baking sheet. Bake for 7–9 minutes until cookies are golden with darker edges. Cool cookies on wire rack.

Cashew Chunk Cookies

Use a good quality chocolate to make these cookies. I prefer breaking a bar of chocolate into chunks rather than buying oversized chips. The combination with whole cashews makes a cookie that is hard to beat!

Preparation time: 25 minutes
Pan: cookie sheets, ungreased
Oven: 350°F. for 10–12 minutes
Yield: 50 cookies

1   cup butter or margarine, softened
1¼ cups brown sugar
1   teaspoon vanilla extract
2   eggs
2¼ cups flour
½   teaspoon baking soda

½   cup cashews, whole or halved
½   cup cashews, finely chopped
2   cups (12 ounces) good quality chocolate or white chocolate chunks

Preheat oven to 350°F.

In a large bowl, cream together brown sugar and butter until light and fluffy. Add the vanilla and beat in the eggs one at a time. Sift flour and baking soda together. Gradually add to the butter mixture. Mix in all the cashews and chocolate chunks. Mix until well blended. Drop by rounded teaspoonfuls onto sheets and bake for 10–12 minutes. Cookies should be lightly browned when done.

Note: If you are looking for a change from chocolate chunk-styled cookies, these are delicious with the cashews only or with the cashews and chopped dried apricots.

Chocolate Chip Crispers

Sweet and chewy! Kids eat these as fast as I can bake them.

Preparation time: 30 minutes
Pan: cookie sheets, greased
Oven: 350°F. for 12 minutes
Yield: 52 cookies

½	cup butter or margarine, softened		1¼	cups all-purpose flour
1	cup granulated sugar		½	teaspoon baking soda
1	egg		¼	teaspoon salt
1	teaspoon vanilla extract		2	cups Rice Crispies®
			1	cup (6 oz.) semisweet chocolate pieces

Preheat oven to 350°F.

In a large bowl, beat butter and sugar until smooth. Beat in the egg and vanilla extract. Set aside.

In a small bowl, combine flour, baking soda, and salt and mix together well.

Add flour mixture to the batter and mix until well-blended. Stir in the Rice Crispies® and chocolate pieces.

Drop by level tablespoonfuls onto greased cookie sheet. Bake about 12 minutes or until light brown. Remove cookies to wire rack to cool.

These freeze well if you can keep them around that long.

Breakfast Cookies

If you're the Danish and donut breakfast type, here is a cookie that will satisfy your sweet tooth as well as put some nutrition into your morning.

Preparation time: 30 minutes
Pan: cookie sheets, lightly greased
Oven: 375°F. for 12–15 minutes
Yield: 36 cookies

1	cup (2 sticks) unsalted butter, softened	½	cup all-purpose flour
½	cup light brown sugar, packed	½	teaspoon baking soda
½	cup granulated sugar	3	cups rolled oats
1	egg	1	cup pitted prunes (packed), chopped
½	teaspoon vanilla extract	½	cup whole natural almonds, chopped
1	cup oat bran		

Preheat oven to 375°F.

In a medium bowl, beat the butter and brown sugar until light and fluffy (about 2 minutes at high speed). Add the granulated sugar and beat for 2 minutes longer. Add the egg and vanilla and blend well.

In another bowl, mix the oat bran, flour and baking soda together. Add to the butter mixture and beat until well blended. Stir in the rolled oats with a wooden spoon (the dough will be coarse and crumbly). Mix in the prunes and almonds.

Scoop up the dough by generous tablespoonfuls, form into balls, and flatten slightly. Place about 1-inch apart, and bake for 12–15 minutes, or until golden. Watch carefully as these tend to get dry if even slightly over baked. Cool cookies on wire racks.

Old-fashioned Chocolate Chip Oatmeal Cookies

Here's a favorite tried-and-true cookie. Young and old alike can never stop at just one of these, so bake enough to freeze some extras.

Preparation time: 35 minutes
Pan: cookie sheets, greased
Oven: 350°F. for 8–10 minutes
Yield: 36 cookies

1	cup (2 sticks) butter or margarine, softened	2	cups flour
1	cup brown sugar	1	teaspoon salt
¾	cup granulated sugar	1	teaspoon baking soda
1	egg, lightly beaten with 1 tablespoon water	1	cup rolled oats
1	teaspoon vanilla extract	2	cups (12 oz.) semisweet chocolate pieces
		½	cup walnuts, chopped

Preheat oven to 350°F.

In a large bowl, cream the butter with both sugars. Add the egg, water and vanilla, beating until fluffy.

Sift the flour, salt, and baking soda together. Blend the sifted ingredients into the creamed mixture. Add the oats, chocolate pieces, and nuts. Blend well.

Drop by teaspoonfuls onto baking sheet. Bake 8–10 minutes until lightly browned. Remove cookies to wire rack to cool.

Loon Mountain Chunks

*My daughter, Elaine, brings these on ski weekends. What a treat!
Needless to say, there are never any left for the trip home.*

Preparation time: 40 minutes
Pan: cookie sheets, greased lightly
Oven: 375°F. for 10–14 minutes
Yield: 36 large cookies

1½ cups hazelnuts
2⅓ cups all-purpose flour
1 teaspoon baking soda
¼ teaspoon salt
1 cup (2 sticks) unsalted butter, softened
1 cup dark brown sugar, packed

½ cup granulated sugar
2 eggs
1 teaspoon vanilla extract
8–9 ounces Hershey's Special Dark Chocolate, broken into ½" chunks
3 teaspoons (1 orange) orange peel

Preheat oven to 375°F.

Spread nuts on baking sheet and bake for 6–8 minutes. Remove nut skins by rubbing nuts in a towel. Coarsely chop nuts and set aside.

In a medium bowl, mix together the flour, baking soda, and salt. In a large bowl, beat the butter until fluffy and creamy (about 3 minutes with electric mixer). Gradually beat in both sugars. Beat in eggs, one at a time, and vanilla. Gradually add the flour mixture, and mix well. Stir in the chocolate, hazelnuts, and orange rind.

Drop by heaping tablespoonfuls onto cookie sheet, about 3" apart. Flatten slightly with a fork. Bake for 10–14 minutes or until lightly browned. Cool cookies on wire rack.

Nut Crisps

Use your favorite nuts for this cookie. Try something different. I've been using pistachios in some batches, pecans in others, and cashews, too.

Preparation time: 30 minutes
Pan: cookie sheets, ungreased
Oven: 325°F. for 15–18 minutes
Yield: 70 cookies

1 cup butter or margarine, softened	2 cups nuts, finely chopped (see note)
⅛ teaspoon salt	1½ cups all-purpose flour, sifted
½ cup powdered sugar, sifted	Powdered sugar
2 teaspoons vanilla extract	

Preheat oven to 325°F.

In large bowl, cream butter with salt until light and fluffy, gradually adding powdered sugar. Add nuts, vanilla, and then flour, blending well. On a lightly floured surface, shape dough into logs, about ½" in diameter. Slice off 1½" pieces. (If dough is too sticky, chill slightly before slicing.) Bake for 15–18 minutes. While cookies are still warm, roll in powdered sugar. Cool completely on wire racks.

Note: You might want to finely chop 1 cup of nuts, and coarsely chop the other cup. This gives nutty flavor throughout, but also the texture of a chunky cookie.

Fresh Apple Cookies

Here is a wonderful moist cookie. The vanilla glaze is optional; I like these without it, but for a sweeter cookie, top with the glaze.

Preparation time: 45 minutes (with glaze) **Yield:** 40 cookies
Pan: cookie sheets, greased
Oven: 400°F. for 10–13 minutes

Cookie dough:
2   cups all-purpose flour, sifted
1   teaspoon baking soda
½   cup butter or margarine
1⅓ cups brown sugar, packed
½   teaspoon salt
1   teaspoon cinnamon
1   teaspoon ground cloves
½   teaspoon nutmeg
1   egg
1   cup chopped nuts

1   cup unpared apple, finely chopped
1   cup raisins, chopped
¼   cup apple juice (or milk)

Vanilla glaze:
1½ cups powdered sugar, sifted
1   tablespoon butter or margarine, softened
¼   teaspoon vanilla extract
⅛   teaspoon salt
2½ tablespoons light cream

Preheat oven to 400°F.
Sift flour and baking soda together. Set aside.
Mix butter, brown sugar, salt, three spices, and egg together until well blended. Stir in half the flour mixture. Add the nuts, apples and raisins. Mix in the apple juice, and then the remaining flour. Blend well. Drop by rounded tablespoonfuls on cookie sheets, 2″ apart. Bake 10–13 minutes. Watch carefully as these should be brown, yet moist. Remove cookies to wire rack and glaze while still hot.
Vanilla glaze: Blend all 5 ingredients together in a small bowl. Lightly glaze cookies while still hot; cookies should be thinly covered rather than frosted.

Peanut Drops

Here's a treat for devoted peanut lovers – a peanutty cookie where the peanut flavor doesn't have to compete with a lot of mix-ins. An added bonus is that these cookies actually taste better after they've been frozen and defrosted.

Preparation time: 35 minutes
Pan: cookie sheets, greased
Oven: 375°F. for 10 minutes
Yield: 100 cookies

1 cup peanut butter, smooth or chunky	1 cup honey
½ cup (1 stick) butter or margarine, softened	2 eggs
2 teaspoons vanilla extract	2½ cups flour
¾ cup granulated sugar	1 teaspoon baking soda
	1 cup salted peanuts, coarsely chopped

Preheat oven to 375°F.

Beat together first 6 ingredients until well blended. Sift flour and soda together. Slowly beat into peanut butter mixture. Mix peanuts in thoroughly. Drop by teaspoonfuls onto cookie sheets, and bake for 8–10 minutes. Watch carefully as these scorch easily, so err on the side of slightly undercooking. Remove cookies to wire rack to cool.

Walnut Surprise

A chewy, nutty cookie that is simply delicious. My favorite for serving with fresh fruit mélange for dessert.

Preparation time: 30 minutes
Pan: cookie sheet, ungreased
Oven: 350°F. for 10 to 12 minutes
Yield: 30 cookies

Pastry:
½   cup butter or margarine, softened
1   cup dark brown sugar, packed
1   egg, well-beaten
½   teaspoon vanilla extract
2¼ cups all-purpose flour
1   teaspoon baking soda
Dash salt

Filling:
¾   cups walnuts, finely chopped
½   cup plus 1 tablespoon brown sugar
¼   cup sour cream

Preheat oven to 350°F.

In a large bowl, cream together the butter and brown sugar. Add the egg and vanilla. Beat well. Sift in the flour, baking soda and salt. Mix until well-blended.

In a small bowl, mix filling ingredients together and set aside.

Drop pastry by teaspoonfuls onto ungreased cookie sheet. Make a well in each cookie with your thumb and add a scant teaspoon of filling to each.

The cookies will flatten as they bake. Bake for 10 to 12 minutes or until they are lightly browned. Cool cookies on wire racks.

These freeze perfectly and are so versatile and popular that I always make a double batch.

Variation: You can substitute pecans for the walnuts. They taste wonderful, but are more expensive.

Spicy Fruit Cookies

A wonderful cookie to bake on an early winter's day. These cookies fill the kitchen with an enticing aroma that beckons all to gather round the kitchen table for cookies and hot cider.

Preparation time: 30 minutes
Pan: cookie sheet, greased
Oven: 375°F. for 10 to 12 minutes
Yield: 70 cookies

1 cup vegetable shortening, softened	3 cups all-purpose flour
1 cup brown sugar, packed	2 teaspoons ground cinnamon
1 egg	1 teaspoon ground cloves
½ cup soured milk (½ cup milk mixed with 1 teaspoon vinegar)	1 teaspoon baking powder
½ cup molasses	1 cup raisins or 1 cup mixture raisins, chopped dates, and chopped prunes
1 teaspoon baking soda (dissolved in the milk)	

Preheat oven to 375°F.

In a large bowl, cream the vegetable shortening. Then add the sugar and egg. Blend well. Add the soured milk and molasses.

Sift the flour with the cinnamon, cloves, and baking powder. Gradually add to the molasses-butter mixture. Stir in raisins or mixed fruit.

Drop by teaspoonfuls on greased cookie sheet. Bake for 10 to 12 minutes until deep brown.

Cool cookies on wire rack. These freeze very well.

Crispy Oatmeal Raisin Cookies

Here's a less chewy oatmeal cookie, bursting with raisins and nuts.

Preparation time: 35 minutes
Pan: cookie sheets, greased
Oven: 400°F. for 10 minutes
Yield: 36 cookies

1½ cups rolled oats, uncooked
½ cup granulated sugar
½ cup butter or margarine, melted
1 egg, beaten
¾ cup all-purpose flour
2 teaspoons baking powder

¼ teaspoon salt
5 teaspoons milk or water
1½ teaspoons vanilla extract
¾ cup seedless raisins
¼ cup nuts, chopped (optional)

Preheat oven to 400°F.

In a large bowl, combine the rolled oats and sugar. Add the melted butter and egg. Mix until well-blended. Set aside.

Sift the flour, baking powder and salt together. Add to the oat mixture, and mix well.

Add the milk, vanilla, raisins, and nuts.

Drop by rounded teaspoonfuls on greased cookie sheet. Press down each spoonful with the back of a wet spoon or fork to about ⅛ inch thickness.

Bake for 10 minutes until lightly browned. Remove to wire rack to cool. These freeze very well.

Oatmeal Shortbread

These can be prepared in a food processor or not, depending on your preference. This cookie dough is so good, you might never get around to baking the cookies!

Preparation time: 15 minutes
Pan: cookie sheets, greased
Oven: 350°F. for 8–12 minutes
Yield: 60 cookies

½	cup nuts	½	cup granulated sugar
2	cups rolled oats, uncooked	¾	cup light brown sugar
1½	cups all-purpose flour	1	egg
½	teaspoon salt	½	teaspoon vanilla extract
1	teaspoon baking soda	½	teaspoon almond extract
1	cup unsalted butter		

Preheat oven to 350°F.

In food processor, chop nuts until very fine. Add rolled oats and blend for 3 seconds. Set aside.

Mix together flour, salt and baking soda.

Process the butter until soft, and then add both sugars. Process until creamed. Add egg and both extracts, blending well. Blend in flour mixture. Add oatmeal-nut mixture and blend.

Roll about 1 tablespoon of dough into ball. Flatten on cookie sheet with a fork. Bake for 8–12 minutes. Remove cookies from sheets and cool on wire racks.

Zucchini Oatmeal Drops

These are crammed with good-for-you ingredients. They make a good breakfast cookie, as well as a nice mid-morning snack.

Preparation time: 30 minutes
Pan: cookie sheet, greased
Oven: 350°F. for 12 minutes
Yield: 50 cookies

½ cup vegetable shortening	1 cup rolled oats, uncooked
1 egg, beaten	½ cup grated zucchini, drained and squeezed dry*
⅛ teaspoon baking soda	
¾ cup honey	½ cup nuts, finely chopped
1 cup all-purpose flour	½ cup seedless raisins
1 teaspoon baking powder	1 teaspoon vanilla extract
Dash salt	

Preheat oven to 350°F.

In a large bowl, cream together the vegetable shortening and egg. Stir the baking soda into the honey, and then add to the creamed ingredients.

Sift the flour, baking powder, and salt together into the creamed mixture.

Combine rolled oats, zucchini, nuts and raisins and stir into batter. Add vanilla extract and blend well.

Drop by rounded teaspoonfuls on greased cookie sheet. Flatten each ball by pressing with a fork. Bake for 12 minutes or until brown. Cool cookies on wire rack.

Variation: Substitute ½ cup grated carrot for the zucchini.

*Note: When zucchini seems to be growing *everywhere*, grate them in your food processor. Squeeze out water. Freeze in 1 cup and ½ cup amounts. Drain and squeeze dry again after defrosting.

Famous Oatmeal Cookies

If you've never tested the recipe on the Quaker Oats® box, here it is – a very fine oatmeal cookie indeed!

Preparation time: 30 minutes
Pan: cookie sheet, greased
Oven: 350°F. for 12 to 15 minutes
Yield: 60 large cookies

¾	cup vegetable shortening	1	teaspoon vanilla extract
1	cup brown sugar, firmly packed	3	cups rolled oats, uncooked
½	cup granulated sugar	1	cup all-purpose flour
1	egg	½	teaspoon baking soda
¼	cup water	½	teaspoon salt (optional)

Preheat oven to 350°F.

In a large bowl, beat together shortening, brown sugar, granulated sugar, egg, water and vanilla extract until creamy. Combine remaining ingredients and add to creamed shortening mixture. Beat well.

Drop by heaping teaspoonfuls (for large cookies) onto greased cookie sheet.

Bake for 12 to 15 minutes or until golden brown. Cool cookies on wire rack. These freeze very well, so I always make a double batch!

Variations: Add ½ cup chopped nuts, raisins, semisweet chocolate pieces or coconut.

Maple Meltaways

If you've never baked with maple syrup before, here is a cookie that will get you hooked. Of course, in Canada and upstate New York, we always used real maple syrup. These bake up to a rich, golden, melt-in-your-mouth delight.

Preparation time: 20 minutes
Pan: cookie sheets, greased
Oven: 350°F. for 8–10 minutes
Yield: 65 cookies

1 cup margarine or butter, softened	1 teaspoon vanilla extract
1 cup brown sugar	4 cups flour
1 egg, lightly beaten	½ teaspoon salt
1 cup maple syrup	2 teaspoons baking powder
	Granulated sugar

Preheat oven to 350°F.

In a large bowl, cream the butter with the brown sugar. Add the egg, syrup and vanilla, beating until well-blended. Mix in the flour, salt, and baking powder. Blend well.

Shape into 1″ balls and roll in some granulated sugar. Flatten slightly. Leave room for cookies to spread. Bake for 8–10 minutes. Remove cookies to wire rack to cool.

Chocolate Chip-Peanut Butter Cookies

This cookie bursts with wonderful flavor. Grind your own peanut butter* for a richer peanutty taste.

Preparation time: 35 minutes
Pan: cookie sheet, ungreased
Oven: 375°F. for 8 to 10 minutes
Yield: 50 cookies

½ cup butter or margarine, softened	1 cup plus 2 tablespoons all-purpose flour
¼ cup granulated sugar	½ teaspoon salt
½ cup brown sugar, firmly packed	½ teaspoon vanilla extract
½ teaspoon baking soda	1 cup smooth or crunchy peanut butter
1 egg, beaten	1 cup (6 oz.) of semisweet chocolate pieces

Preheat oven to 375°F.

In a large bowl, cream together butter, sugar, and brown sugar. Add the remaining ingredients in the order shown, and mix until well-blended.

Drop by rounded teaspoonfuls onto an ungreased cookie sheet. Bake for 8 to 10 minutes or until golden brown. Remove to wire racks to cool.

*2 cups peanuts to 1 tablespoon peanut oil. Blend in your food processor on high until smooth or crunchy, whichever you prefer.

Original Toll House® Cookies

Some recipes simply cannot be improved upon . . . here is the all-time favorite chocolate chip cookie.

Preparation time: 20 minutes
Pan: cookie sheet, ungreased
Oven: 375°F. for 8 to 10 minutes
Yield: 100 cookies

1	cup butter or margarine, softened	1	teaspoon baking soda
¾	cup granulated sugar	1	teaspoon salt
¾	cup brown sugar, firmly packed	2	cups (12 oz.) semisweet chocolate pieces
2	eggs	1	cup chopped nuts (optional)
2¼	cups all-purpose flour	1	teaspoon vanilla extract

Preheat oven to 375°F.

In a large bowl beat butter, sugar, brown sugar, vanilla extract and eggs together until a fluffy batter forms. Set aside.

Sift together flour, baking soda and salt. Add to batter, beating until well-blended. Mix in the chocolate pieces and nuts.

Drop by rounded teaspoonfuls on ungreased cookie sheets.

Bake for 8 to 10 minutes or until lightly browned. Cool cookies on wire racks.

Chocolate Chip Meringue Kisses

These puffs of sweetness are wonderful holiday cookies. You can set them out on a silver dish like candy or pass them around at dessert time with coffee and tea.

Preparation time: 10 minutes
Pan: cookie sheet
Oven: 300°F. for 25 minutes
Yield: 36 cookies

2 egg whites (room temperature)	¾ teaspoon vanilla extract
⅛ teaspoon salt	¾ cup granulated sugar
⅛ teaspoon cream of tartar	1 cup (6 oz.) semisweet chocolate pieces

Preheat oven to 300°F. Line cookie sheet with a brown paper bag.

In a medium bowl, beat egg whites, salt, cream of tartar and vanilla extract together until smooth.

Gradually add the sugar and continue beating until batter forms peaks. Fold in the chocolate pieces.

Drop by teaspoonfuls onto lined cookie sheet. Swirl the top to look like a big chocolate kiss.

Bake for 25 minutes. Cool on wire rack. If you plan to freeze these, be sure not to crowd, as they break quite easily.

Cocoa-Pecan Drops

These are very rich, but not too sweet. The cream cheese filling brings out the best in the pecans.

Preparation time: 45 minutes
Pan: cookie sheets, ungreased
Oven: 350°F. for 10 to 12 minutes
Yield: 50 cookies

Dough:
1   cup butter, softened
1   cup powdered sugar
2   tablespoons unsweetened cocoa
1¾ cups all-purpose flour, sifted
1   egg yolk (reserve white)

Filling:
1   cup powdered sugar
1   egg yolk (reserve white)
3   tablespoons unsweetened cocoa
6   ounces (2 small packages) cream cheese, softened
1¼ teaspoons vanilla extract

Garnish:
2   egg whites
1½ cups pecans, chopped
50   pecan halves
     Preheat oven to 350°F.

In a large bowl, cream the butter and add remaining dough ingredients. Mix until very well-blended. Set aside.

In a small bowl, combine 1 cup powdered sugar and cream cheese. Cream and add remaining filling ingredients. Mix until smooth. Set aside.

Beat 2 egg whites until foamy. Set aside.

Roll dough into 50 walnut-sized balls. Dip each ball into the egg whites and then roll in chopped pecans. Place about 1 inch apart on cookie sheet. Press thumb into center of each ball, making a well. Drop 1 teaspoon of filling in each well. Adorn with pecan half.

Bake for 10 to 12 minutes. Cool on sheets for 3 minutes and remove to wire rack to complete cooling. Store in refrigerator.

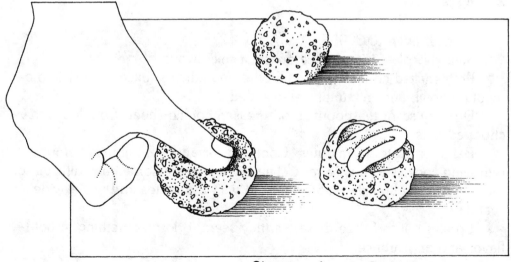

Shaping Cocoa-Pecan Drops

Chocolate Thinsees

These are a small, lightly flavored tea cookie. But watch out – they can be very habit-forming.

Preparation time: 30 minutes
Pan: cookie sheet, greased
Oven: 300°F. for 10 to 12 minutes
Yield: 70 small cookies

2 squares semisweet chocolate, melted	Dash of salt
½ cup butter, softened	½ cup all-purpose flour
1 cup brown sugar, packed	¼ teaspoon vanilla extract
2 eggs	¾ cup nuts, finely chopped

Preheat oven to 300°F.

Melt chocolate in a double boiler or microwave.

Pour melted chocolate and all other ingredients (except nuts) into a medium bowl, and mix until well-blended

Drop by scant teaspoonfuls on greased cookie sheet. Sprinkle with chopped nuts.

Bake for 10 to 12 minutes. Cool pan for about 2 minutes before removing cookies to a wire rack. These cookies are sometimes difficult to remove without breaking, so be sure to wait 2 minutes and use a wide spatula.

I prefer not to freeze these, as they seem to lose something in both flavor and appearance.

Honey-Raisin Meltaways

A subtle melding of honey, brown sugar and almond flavors afloat in a light fluffy batter.

Preparation time: 25 minutes
Pan: cookie sheet, greased
Oven: 375°F. for 10 to 12 minutes
Yield: 36 cookies

¼	cup butter or margarine, softened	1	cup all-purpose flour, pre-sifted
⅓	cup brown sugar, packed	1	teaspoon baking powder
⅓	cup honey	1	teaspoon almond extract
2	eggs, separated	3	tablespoons milk
		1	cup seedless raisins

Preheat oven to 375°F.

In a large bowl, cream the butter and sugar together. Add the honey and egg yolks. Mix until well-blended. Set aside egg whites, and mix in all remaining ingredients.

Beat egg whites until they form stiff peaks. Gently fold into batter with a wooden spoon.

Drop by teaspoonfuls onto greased cookie sheets. Bake for 10 to 12 minutes. Remove to wire racks to cool. These freeze very well.

Sugar Cookies

I baked these on a wood cookstove when we lived in Jasper, New York, 40 years ago. This is still the best sugar cookie recipe I've found.

Preparation time: 25 minutes
Pan: cookie sheets, greased
Oven: 350°F. for 12 to 15 minutes
Yield: 120 cookies

1 cup vegetable shortening	1¼ cups soured milk (mix 1 cup milk with 2 tablespoons vinegar)
2 cups granulated sugar	
2 eggs	1 teaspoon vanilla extract or lemon juice concentrate
3 cups all-purpose flour	
1 teaspoon baking powder	Raisins, chopped dates, chopped walnuts, or shredded coconut (optional)
1 teaspoon baking soda	

Preheat oven to 350°F.

In a large bowl, cream the shortening. Add the sugar and eggs, and blend in thoroughly. Set aside.

Sift the flour and the baking powder into a medium bowl. Set aside.

Mix the baking soda with the soured milk.

To the shortening mixture, alternately stir in the flour mixture and the milk mixture. Add the vanilla extract and any optional ingredients you wish. Mix all thoroughly.

Drop by heaping teaspoonfuls onto greased cookie sheet. Bake for 12 to 15 minutes. Sprinkle with some granulated sugar or colored sugar crystals while still warm. Remove to wire rack to cool. These freeze very well.

Coffee Cookies

A mild coffee flavor in a cookie that is not too sweet.

Preparation time: 30 minutes
Pan: cookie sheet, greased
Oven: 350°F. for 10 to 12 minutes
Yield: 30 cookies

½ cup vegetable shortening	¾ cup all-purpose flour
⅔ cup granulated sugar	½ teaspoon vanilla extract
2 tablespoons (powdered) instant coffee	½ cup nuts, chopped (optional)
1 egg	

Preheat oven to 350°F.

In a medium bowl, cream together the shortening, sugar and instant coffee. Add the remaining ingredients and mix until well-blended.

Drop by rounded teaspoonfuls on greased cookie sheet. Bake for 10 to 12 minutes. Remove cookies immediately from pan and cool on a wire rack.

Variation 1: *Mocha Cookies.* Add 3 tablespoons of powdered cocoa to the batter for a rich mocha flavor.

Variation 2: *Coffee-Amaretto Cookies.* Substitute ½ teaspoon almond extract for the vanilla extract and add ½ cup toasted slivered almonds. Or add 1 teaspoon amaretto liqueur and ½ cup toasted slivered almonds. Omit the vanilla extract.

Cream Cheese Kisses

Take a rich cream cheese batter; add the tartness of lemon, the subtlety of pecans and you have a wonderfully balanced, very fine cookie.

Preparation time: 20 minutes
Pan: cookie sheets, ungreased
Oven: 300°F for 20 minutes
Yield: 60 cookies

¾ cup butter or margarine, softened	2 teaspoons grated lemon peel
1 (3 oz.) package cream cheese, softened	1 teaspoon vanilla extract
1 cup powdered sugar	2 cups all-purpose flour
1 tablespoon lemon juice	1 cup pecans, finely chopped
	Powdered sugar, sifted

Preheat oven to 300°F.

In a large bowl, beat the butter and cream cheese until light and fluffy. Gradually add 1 cup powdered sugar and beat at high speed for 1 minute.

Reduce speed and mix in lemon juice, lemon peel and vanilla extract. Add the flour, and mix well. Stir in the chopped nuts.

Drop by teaspoonfuls onto ungreased cookie sheet. Bake 20 minutes, until lightly browned.

While still hot, either roll in or sprinkle with powdered sugar.

Cool on wire racks.

Peanut Butter Surprises

Here's a treat and then some . . . peanut butter plus crunchy peanuts plus chocolate pieces, all in a brown sugar cookie. These cookies get eaten so fast that you'd better always bake a double batch.

Preparation time: 30 minutes
Pan: cookie sheets, ungreased
Oven: 350°F. for 8 to 10 minutes
Yield: 100 cookies

2	cups all-purpose flour	2	eggs
2	teaspoons baking soda	1¼	teaspoons vanilla extract
½	teaspoon salt	1	cup peanut butter*
1	cup butter or margarine, softened	¾	cup peanuts, unsalted
1	cup granulated sugar	1	cup (6 oz.) package semisweet chocolate pieces
1¼	cups light brown sugar, firmly packed		

Preheat oven to 350°F.

Into a medium bowl, sift together flour, soda and salt. Set aside.

In a large bowl, cream the butter and both sugars until light. Add the eggs and vanilla extract; beat until light and fluffy.

Blend in the peanut butter. Gradually add the flour mixture. Stir in the peanuts and chocolate pieces.

Drop by teaspoonfuls onto ungreased cookie sheets. Bake for 8 to 10 minutes or until lightly browned.

Remove cookies to wire racks to cool.

Variations: Substitute butterscotch pieces for chocolate pieces or add raisins to the batter.

Helen's Christmas Cookies

Helen is ninety-five years old and she still bakes these for her family every Christmas. They will rival fruit cake in popularity, and will be year 'round favorites.

Preparation time: 30 minutes
Pan: cookie sheets, greased
Oven: 300°F. for 30 minutes
Yield: 72 cookies

3 cups all-purpose flour	1 small (6 oz.) jar maraschino cherries, chopped (reserve liquid)
1 teaspoon baking soda	
½ teaspoon salt	
1 cup vegetable shortening	1 (8 oz.) package dates, coarsely chopped
1½ cups granulated sugar	
3 eggs	½ cup walnuts, coarsely chopped

Preheat oven to 300°F.

In a large bowl, sift together flour, baking soda, and salt. Set aside.

In a small bowl, mix the cherries, dates and walnuts together. Pour the cherry juice over the mixture. Set aside.

Cream together the shortening and sugar. Add the eggs and blend well. Add the cherry-date mixture and mix until well-blended.

Add the creamed-cherry batter to the flour mixture and blend well.

Drop by rounded teaspoonfuls on greased cookie sheet. Bake for 30 minutes. Remove cookies to wire rack to cool.

These freeze very well.

Chocolate Macaroons

A chewy coconut treat. In the summer, these are good cold from the refrigerator, or partially frozen.

Preparation time: 25 minutes
Pan: cookie sheets, greased
Oven: 325°F. for 20 minutes
Yield: 35 macaroons

3	egg whites	1½	cups semisweet chocolate pieces, melted
¾	cup granulated sugar, sifted	2¼	cups shredded coconut
⅜	teaspoon salt	½	cup finely chopped walnuts or pecans (optional)
1	teaspoon vanilla extract		

Preheat oven to 325°F.

In a large bowl, beat egg whites until foamy. Add salt and beat a little more.

Gradually add sugar, a tablespoon at a time, beating constantly until mixture stands in peaks. Add vanilla. Fold in cooled melted chocolate. Add coconut and nuts.

Mix gently. Drop in small mounds by teaspoonfuls on a greased cookie sheet.

Bake for 15 to 20 minutes. Do not overbake. Cookies must still be slightly soft in center. Remove pan to wire rack. Cool a few minutes and then use a spatula to loosen cookies from pan.

These freeze very well.

Lacey Wafers

Mildly flavored, these delicate cookies are perfect when served with fresh fruit and dessert cheeses.

Preparation time: 20 minutes
Pan: cookie sheets, lined with foil
Oven: 325°F. for 8 to 10 minutes
Yield: 24 cookies

¼	cup light corn syrup	½	cup all-purpose flour, presifted
¼	cup brown sugar, firmly packed	¾	cup pecans, finely chopped
¼	cup butter or margarine, softened	½	teaspoon vanilla extract

Preheat oven to 325°F, and line cookie sheets with foil.

In a small saucepan, combine syrup, sugar and butter. Cook over medium heat, stirring constantly, until mixture comes to a boil. Take care not to scorch.

Remove from heat, and add flour and nuts. Mix until well-blended. Add vanilla extract and mix well.

Drop onto foiled cookie sheets by teaspoonfuls, about 3 inches apart. Bake 8 to 10 minutes until golden brown.

Cool pan on wire rack. When cookies are thoroughly cooled, peel cookies off foil. Store in airtight containers.

4

Golde's
One, Two, Three Cookies

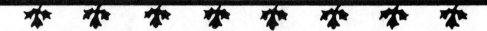

I call these One, Two, Three Cookies for two reasons. The first is that most of these recipes are very easy; the only tricky part is planning your time, and even that can be quite flexible. They really are as easy as one, two, three.

The second reason is that all of these recipes call for chilling the batter or dough for at least half an hour, or as long as overnight. So there are three steps: a time for preparing batter; a time to chill batter; a time to bake cookies. Each step takes very little time, and when all is said and done (if you plan your baking around your natural schedule and not the other way around), these cookies seem to prepare themselves. Though I've said it before, it's especially pertinent to these recipes . . . plan your time ahead.

FLEXIBILITY PLUS!

These recipes have a great deal of flexibility in them, so take advantage of that. In fact, most every recipe here can be started in your spare time and completed when it suits your schedule. Once your dough is prepared, you have the option of

- chilling your dough for specified time in the refrigerator and then baking;
- wrapping it *well*, and refrigerating overnight or even for a few days;
- wrapping dough with freezer wrap, and freezing for as long as a month or two.

As you can see, these recipes are time-efficient for even the busiest schedules.

GOLDE'S PREPARE NOW . . . BAKE LATER METHOD

My family teases me because I take organization so seriously, but for me it makes baking easier and more enjoyable. I say that I simply never leave anything to chance, that good organization results in better prepared cookies and eliminates costly errors.

Since I usually bake in the morning I get *everything* ready the night before. For you, it might mean getting things ready when you first get home in the late afternoon, so you can bake later that night or the next evening.

Here's what I do in preparation:
- read recipe through completely
- take all ingredients out
- take out all pans, and utensils I'll need
- measure dry ingredients such as sugar or flour
- group (in the refrigerator) all other ingredients I'll be using
- put out on counter any ingredients used for decoration or garnishes

Now I'm set to go first thing in the morning. Preparation time is reduced and so are errors. I put everything away as I use it. If I need 1 teaspoon vanilla extract, the bottle goes back into the cupboard as soon as I add the teaspoonful to the batter. That way I never put an ingredient in twice, and never omit it entirely.

I urge everyone who can't find the time to bake cookies to try this "prepare-ahead . . . bake-later" method on a basic refrigerator cookie. You'll see that it really works!

Chinese Almond Cakes

Easy and very good! Bake them once and they will quickly become family favorites.

Preparation time: 15 minutes   **Refrigerate:** 30 minutes

1½ cups all-purpose flour	¾ cup granulated sugar
½ teaspoon baking powder	1 egg
¼ teaspoon salt	1 teaspoon almond extract
½ cup (1 stick) butter or margarine	

Sift flour, baking powder, and salt together. Set aside. Cream butter and sugar together until light and fluffy. Beat in egg and almond extract. Place dough on well-floured surface, and knead 5 to 6 strokes or until smooth. Shape into a flattened round. Wrap in waxed paper and refrigerate 30 minutes.

Final preparation time: 15 minutes
Pan: cookie sheets, lightly greased
Oven: 350°F. for 12–15 minutes
Yield: 18 cookies

Whole almonds, blanched   1 egg, beaten

Preheat oven to 350°F.
Divide dough in half. Cut each half into 9 equal-sized pieces, shaping each piece into a ball. Place on cookie sheets and flatten ball. Press an almond in center of each cookie and brush cookie tops with beaten egg. Bake about 12–15 minutes or until golden. Cool cookies on wire racks.

Mint Surprises

This is a perfect cookie to go with coffee, tea or a tall glass of milk.
Teenagers can consume a whole batch in one sitting!

Preparation time: 20 minutes

Refrigerate: 2 hours or overnight

½	cup (1 stick) butter or margarine, softened
⅓	cup granulated sugar
¼	cup brown sugar, firmly packed
1	egg

1½	teaspoons water
½	teaspoon vanilla extract
1½	cups flour
½	teaspoon baking soda
½	teaspoon salt

In a large bowl, cream butter, gradually adding both sugars. Beat in egg, water and vanilla. Sift together flour, baking soda and salt. Blend into butter mixture. Wrap in waxed paper and chill at least 2 hours.

Final preparation time: 15 minutes
Pan: cookie sheets, greased
Oven: 375°F. for 10–12 minutes
Yield: 24 cookies

24	chocolate-covered thin mints
24	pecan halves

Preheat oven to 375°F.

Surround each thin mint with 1 tablespoon dough. (The mints can be cut in half for a smaller cookie.) Place on cookie sheet and top with pecan. Bake at 375° for 10–12 minutes until lightly browned. Let stand 1 minute before removing from pan to cool on wire racks.

Poppy Seed Rounds

A not-too-sweet cookie for the more sophisticated palate, Poppy Seed Rounds are an especially attractive addition to any platter of cookies.

Preparation time: 15 minutes   **Refrigerate:** 30–60 minutes

Dough:
1½ cups butter or margarine, softened	2 teaspoons vanilla extract
1 cup granulated sugar	¼ teaspoon salt
1 egg	4½ cups flour

Beat butter, sugar, egg, vanilla and salt together until light and fluffy. Gradually add flour and beat until well mixed. Cover dough and chill for 30–60 minutes.

Final preparation time: 20 minutes
Pan: cookie sheets, ungreased
Oven: 375°F. for 8–10 minutes
Yield: 50 cookies

1   egg, beaten   Poppy seeds

Preheat oven to 375°F.
Work with ¼ dough at a time, keeping the remaining dough chilled. Roll dough out between 2 pieces of waxed paper to ¼" thick. Cut out with donut cutter (or other shapes if you choose). Reroll trimmings for no waste. Place on cookie sheets, and brush with beaten egg. Sprinkle lightly with poppy seeds. Bake for 8–10 minutes or until cookies are lightly browned. Cool cookies on wire racks.

Ribbon Cookies

If you like chocolate-cherry combinations, here's a wonderful cookie for you.

Preparation time: 30 minutes
Pan: 9" × 5" × 3" loaf pan

Refrigerate: 24 hours

2½ cups all-purpose flour	1 teaspoon vanilla extract
1½ teaspoons baking powder	¼ cup snipped candied cherries
½ teaspoon salt	
1 cup butter or margarine, softened	1 square unsweetened chocolate, melted
1¼ cups granulated sugar	2 tablespoons poppy seeds
1 egg	

Sift flour with baking powder and salt. In a large bowl, cream butter until fluffy, gradually adding sugar. Beat egg and vanilla into creamed butter mixture. Blend in flour mixture.

Divide dough into 3 parts, adding cherries to one part, chocolate to the second part, and the poppy seeds to the third. Line loaf pan with waxed paper. Pack cherry dough in bottom, then chocolate dough as middle layer, and poppy seed mixture as top layer. Cover with waxed paper and refrigerate at least 24 hours.

Final preparation time: 10 minutes
Pan: cookie sheets, ungreased

Oven: 400°F. for 8–10 minutes
Yield: 75 cookies

Preheat oven to 400°F. Remove dough from pan. Cut loaf in half lengthwise. Slice crosswise into ½"–¾" slices. Bake 8–10 minutes or until light brown. Cool on wire rack.

Hugs and Kisses

Chocolate kisses surrounded by light cookie dough – fun for the children to make, fun for all to eat. These are also good with fruit fillings – cherries and dates work well.

Preparation time: 10 minutes　　　**Refrigerate:** 1 hour

1　cup (2 sticks) butter or margarine	1　teaspoon vanilla extract
½　cup granulated sugar	2　cups flour

Cream butter with sugar until light and fluffy. Add vanilla and flour. Mix well. Chill dough at least 1 hour.

Final preparation time: 10 minutes
Pan: cookie sheets, ungreased
Oven: 375°F. for 12–15 minutes
Yield: 60 cookies

1　bag (14 ounces) chocolate kisses　　　Powdered sugar

Preheat oven to 375°F.

Break off a piece of dough, roll into a ball and flatten with palm of your hand. Dough should not be too thick. Place chocolate kiss in center and bring dough up, shaping it to cover kiss completely.

Bake in 375°F. oven for 12–15 minutes until just lightly brown. Cool cookies on wire racks. Roll in powdered sugar, if you wish. (They are plenty sweet without this.)

Lemon Thins

A light, delicate cookie. Alter the amount of lemon peel to suit your taste.

Preparation time: 20 minutes

Refrigerate: 30 minutes or overnight

1	cup (2 sticks) butter or margarine, softened
½	cup granulated sugar
1	egg, beaten
2	cups sifted flour

½	teaspoon baking powder
⅛	teaspoon salt
1½	tablespoons lemon juice
1	teaspoon grated lemon peel

Cream butter and sugar together. Add the egg and blend well. Sift flour, baking powder and salt. Add to other mixture. Stir in lemon juice and peel. Form into logs, 1½″ to 2″ in diameter. Work with floured hands. (Add additional flour if dough is too sticky.) Wrap logs in waxed paper and refrigerate at least 30 minutes.

Final preparation time: 5 minutes
Pan: cookie sheets, ungreased
Oven: 375°F. for 8–10 minutes
Yield: 70 cookies

Preheat oven to 375°F.
Slice logs into very thin cookies. Bake 8–10 minutes. (If your oven tends to run hot, set at 350°F.) Cool cookies on wire rack.

Macadamia Bars

Extraordinarily delicious!

Preparation time: 30 minutes
Pan: 10″ × 15″ jelly-roll pan

Refrigeration: 30 minutes or longer

2½ cups all-purpose flour
2 tablespoons granulated sugar
1 cup (2 sticks) butter

6–7 tablespoons cold water
½ teaspoon vanilla extract

In a large bowl mix flour and sugar together. Cut in butter until mixture resembles coarse crumbs. Add water and vanilla, and mix until a ball forms. On a lightly floured surface, roll dough out to 8″ × 13″. Press on bottom and sides of jelly-roll pan. Refrigerate at least 30 minutes.

Final preparation time: 20 minutes
Oven: 400°F. for 10 minutes (pastry)
350°F. for 50–55 minutes (filling)

Yield: 50–60 cookies

Filling:
2 cups heavy cream
¼ cup rum or flavoring
1½ cups granulated sugar
¼ teaspoon salt
1 teaspoon vanilla extract
14 oz. salted macadamia nuts, coarsely chopped

Preheat oven to 400°F.

Bake refrigerated pastry for 10 minutes. Cool pan, lower oven temperature to 350°F. and prepare filling. Bring all ingredients, except nuts, to a boil over medium-high heat. Stir constantly to avoid scorching, and boil 10 minutes. Add nuts and cook for 5 minutes more. Pour filling into crust. Bake for 50–55 minutes. Cookies should be golden brown. Cool pan before cutting into bars.

Jam Swirls

There are many variations on this recipe, but I still prefer my long-time favorite because it's very good and very attractive.

Preparation time: 15 minutes   **Refrigerate:** several hours

½	cup (1 stick) butter or margarine, softened	1	egg
1	cup granulated sugar	2	cups flour
1	teaspoon vanilla extract	1	teaspoon baking powder
		¼	teaspoon salt

Beat butter, sugar, vanilla and egg together until light and fluffy. Sift together flour, baking powder, and salt. Beat into butter mixture until well blended. Refrigerate dough until firm, several hours or overnight.

Preparation time: 10 minutes   **Refrigerate:** several hours

½	cup jam (seedless)	¼	cup nuts, finely chopped
¼	cup coconut		

Bring dough to room temperature. On a lightly floured surface, roll dough out to 9″ × 12″ size. Mix jam, nuts, and coconut together. Spread over dough to ½″ of edges. Roll dough jelly-roll style. Cut the log in half. Wrap in waxed paper and refrigerate again for several hours or overnight.

Final preparation time: 5 minutes   **Oven:** 375°F. for 8–10 minutes
Pan: cookie sheets, greased   **Yield:** 45 cookies

Preheat oven to 375°F.
Slice logs into ¼″ cookie slices and place 2″ apart on sheets. Bake 8–10 minutes until golden. Cool on wire racks.

Cinnamon Crescents

My husband, David's, favorites. These take a little extra effort, but it's well worth it for these pastry-like cookies. Good for breakfast or brunch, too!

Preparation time: 15 minutes
Refrigerate: 3 hours

Pastry:
1	package (¼ oz.) dry yeast
¼	cup water, lukewarm
3	cups flour, sifted

2½ tablespoons granulated sugar
1 cup (2 sticks) butter or margarine, softened
2 eggs, lightly beaten

Melt butter. Beat the two eggs.

In a large bowl, sprinkle the yeast on the warm water and stir to dissolve.

Add the sifted flour. Add the sugar, melted butter and beaten eggs. Mix until well-blended.

Cover the bowl tightly and refrigerate for 3 hours or overnight. (The dough can be stored up to 3 days in the refrigerator.)

Final preparation time: 1 hour
Pan: cookie sheet, ungreased
Oven: 350°F. for 15 minutes
Yield: 48 cookies

Filling:

½   **cup granulated sugar**

1   **tablespoon ground cinnamon**

When ready to bake, preheat oven to 350°F.

Mix the sugar and cinnamon together and set aside.

Divide the pastry dough into 6 or 7 parts.

Take an 8- or 9-inch pie pan, and sprinkle it well with some of the filling mixture. Roll out one part of dough and press into pie pan. Sprinkle generously again with filling mixture.

Cut dough into 8 wedges, as you would a pie. Roll each wedge starting at widest end, as you would a crescent roll.

Let crescents stand 15 minutes before baking. Then place on ungreased cookie sheet, and bake for 15 minutes or until lightly golden. Remove cookies to cool on wire racks.

Repeat until all 6 or 7 dough balls are used. These freeze very well.

Variation: Before rolling into crescents, spread your favorite jam sparingly, or finely chopped nuts, or chopped raisins onto pastry dough, along with the sugar-cinnamon filling mixture.

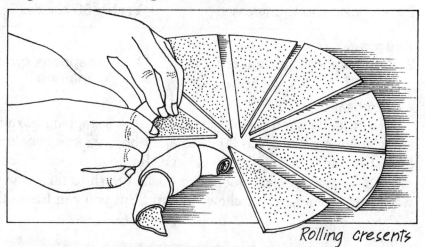

Rolling cresents

Mrs. Vincent's Snickerdoodles

A favorite of all my daughters because Mrs. Vincent always let them feast on these cinnamon gems – fresh out of the oven.

Preparation time: 20 minutes   **Refrigeration:** 2 hours

2¾ cups all-purpose flour
2   teaspoons cream of tartar
1   teaspoon baking soda
½   teaspoon salt

1   cup vegetable shortening, softened
1½ cups granulated sugar
2   eggs

In a large bowl, sift together flour, cream of tartar, baking soda and salt.

Cream shortening, sugar and eggs until light and fluffy. (Use electric mix master on medium speed or cream with spoon.)

Beat flour mixture (at low speed) into creamed ingredients until a dough-like batter forms. Chill for two hours, until easy to handle.

Final preparation time: 15 minutes   **Oven:** 400°F. for 8 to 10 minutes
Pan: cookie sheet, ungreased   **Yield:** 60 cookies

Topping:
2   tablespoons granulated sugar

2   teaspoons ground cinnamon

Preheat oven to 400°F.

Form dough into walnut-sized balls. Roll in topping mixture of sugar and cinnamon. Place balls 2-inches apart on ungreased cookie sheet. Bake 8 to 10 minutes or until lightly colored. Remove cookies to cool.

These are especially good when baked fresh to take advantage of the wonderful aroma and the chewy texture. But you can freeze them if you wish.

Favorite Peanut Butter Cookies

Peanut butter cookies are the unheralded but much-loved favorites of many, many people.

Preparation time: 15 minutes
Refrigerate: 1 hour or longer

1	cup brown sugar, packed	2	cups all-purpose flour
1	cup granulated sugar	1	teaspoon salt
1	cup butter or margarine, softened	1	teaspoon baking soda
1	cup peanut butter	1	teaspoon baking powder
2	eggs	1	teaspoon vanilla extract

In a large bowl, cream together the brown sugar, granulated sugar, butter, peanut butter and eggs until well-blended.

Sift the dry ingredients and add to the creamed batter. Add the vanilla extract. Mix well. Chill dough thoroughly.

Final preparation time: 15 minutes
Pan: cookie sheet, greased
Oven: 350°F. for 10 to 12 minutes
Yield: 95 cookies

When ready to bake, preheat oven to 350°F.

Break dough into walnut-sized pieces. Press these with a fork onto greased cookie sheet.

Bake for 10 to 12 minutes. Remove to wire rack and cool. These freeze very well.

Mock Streudel Slices

A light pastry bursting with apricots, raisins, nuts and coconut.
This is easier than it looks and oh-so-delicious!

Preparation time: 5 minutes
Refrigerate: overnight

Pastry:

1 cup (2 sticks) butter or margarine, softened	1½ cups all-purpose flour
	½ cup sour cream

In a medium bowl, cut the butter into the flour until mixed and crumbly. Stir in the sour cream until blended. Divide the dough into four equal parts. Wrap each in waxed paper or plastic wrap. Refrigerate overnight or several days.

Final preparation time: 10 minutes
Pan: 15" × 10" jelly-roll pan, greased
Oven: 350°F. for 20 to 25 minutes
Yield: 32 pieces

Fruit Coconut Filling:

1 jar (10 oz.) apricot preserves	½ cup walnuts, chopped
	½ cup flaked coconut
½ cup white seedless raisins	⅓ cup powdered sugar, sifted

When ready to bake, preheat oven to 350°F.

Roll the pastry dough (one at a time) out onto a well-floured board into a rectangular shape, about 11" × 7".

Spread with ¼ of the apricot preserves. Sprinkle with raisins, nuts and coconut.

Turn up three times as you would a jelly-roll, starting from the bottom and rolling over. Place on a greased jelly roll pan (2 streudels to a pan), and bake for 20 to 25 minutes until lightly golden. Remove pan to wire rack and cool for 5 minutes before slicing into 1-inch slices. When slices are cool, sprinkle with sifted powdered sugar. These freeze very well.

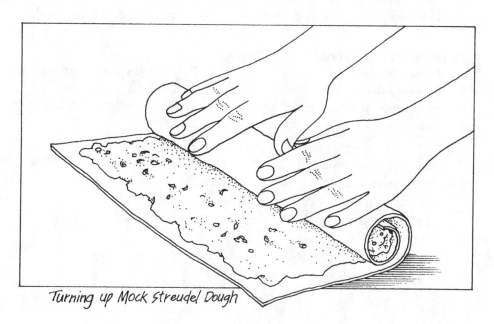

Turning up Mock Streudel Dough

Streudel Fillings

Date Filling

3	cups diced dates
¼	cup granulated sugar

1½　cups water

Lemon juice to taste

Mix all ingredients together in a saucepan.

Cook over low heat, stirring constantly, until thickened (about 10 minutes).

Cool. Proceed to fill pastry.

This may be made 2 or 3 days in advance. Keep refrigerated.

Orange-Prune Streudel Filling:

3　cups steamed or cooked prunes, diced and drained

¼　to ½ cup granulated sugar

½　cup orange juice

2　tablespoons grated orange rind

Grated rind and juice of ½ lemon

Mix all ingredients together in a saucepan. Cook over low heat, stirring constantly until thickened, about 10 minutes.

Cool thoroughly. Proceed to spread over pastry.

This may be made 2 or 3 days before using. Keep refrigerated.

Pecan Tarts

The light cream cheese pastry and pecan filling make this tart superb. These are perfect served on a tray to pass at dessert time — especially if you are serving fresh fruit, sherbet or ice cream.

Preparation time: 5 minutes   **Refrigerate:** 1 hour

Pastry:

1	small (3 oz.) package of cream cheese	½	cup butter, softened
		1	cup flour

Blend butter and cream cheese together. Then add flour, and mix until dough is formed. Chill in refrigerator at least 1 hour.

Final preparation time: 40 minutes   **Oven:** 325°F. for 25 minutes
Pan: small tart tins, ungreased   **Yield:** 24 tarts

Filling:

¾	cup brown sugar	1	tablespoon butter
1	teaspoon vanilla extract		Dash of salt
1	egg	⅔	cup pecans, coarsely chopped

When ready to bake, preheat oven to 325°F.

Shape refrigerated pastry dough into 24 1-inch balls (walnut-sized). Place in small ungreased tart tins (no paper liners). Press dough around bottom and sides.

Beat all filling ingredients (except pecans) together until smooth.

Place ⅓ cup of pecans on top of pressed pastry dough. Add 1 tablespoon of filling to each tart cup. Sprinkle remaining ⅓ cup of pecans over filling. Bake for 25 minutes until set

Remove and cool on wire rack. These freeze well, although they are somewhat delicate and need to be packed carefully.

Golde's Basic Butter Refrigerator Cookies

A sweet cookie batter which is ideal for adding nuts, fruits, chocolate pieces – make ahead, bake later!

Preparation time: 10 minutes   **Refrigerate:** about 3 hours or longer

½ cup butter, softened	1 teaspoon vanilla extract
1 cup granulated sugar	¾ cup chopped nuts, raisins,
1 egg, beaten	dates, chocolate pieces,
1¾ cups all-purpose flour	sunflower seeds or
2 teaspoons baking powder	coconut (optional)
¼ teaspoon salt	

In a large bowl, cream together the butter and sugar. Add the beaten egg. Sift the flour, baking powder and salt together. Beat the flour mixture into the creamed mixture. Add vanilla extract and any optional of ingredients you choose.

Shape the dough into two rolls, 2-inches thick and about 12-inches long. Wrap each in plastic wrap or waxed paper and refrigerate until well-chilled (or wrap in freezer wrap and freeze up to 3 months).

Final preparation time: 5 minutes   **Oven:** 375°F. for 8 to 10 minutes
Pans: cookie sheet, lightly greased   **Yield:** 96 cookies

When ready to bake, preheat oven to 375°F.

Cut rolls into thin (about ⅛-inch) slices, and bake on lightly greased cookie sheets for about 8 to 10 minutes or until golden brown. Remove cookies to cool on wire racks.

You can freeze these after baking, as well as before baking.

Brown Sugar Refrigerator Cookies

This dough can be made in advance and frozen in 2-inch × 12-inch rolls for the quickest homemade cookies ever.

Preparation time: 15 minutes   **Refrigerate:** 3 hours

1	cup butter or margarine, softened	2	cups all-purpose flour
½	cup brown sugar, packed	½	teaspoon baking soda
½	cup granulated sugar	½	teaspoon vanilla extract
1	egg, beaten slightly	½	cup nuts, chopped

In a large bowl, cream the butter, brown sugar, and granulated sugar. Add the beaten egg. Sift the flour and baking soda together. Add sifted flour to the creamed mixture; then add the vanilla and nuts.

Shape the dough with your hands into 2-inch thick rolls, about 12-inches long.

Refrigerate rolls for several hours, or wrap in freezer wrap and freeze for future baking.

Final preparation time: 5 minutes   **Oven:** 375°F. for 8 to 10 minutes
Pan: cookie sheet, greased   **Yield:** 96 cookies

When ready to bake, preheat oven to 375°F.

Slice into ¼-inch thick slices, and place on lightly greased cookie sheet. Bake for 8 to 10 minutes until golden. Remove cookies to wire rack to cool.

These freeze well after baking, too, but be sure to pack loosely.

Serving suggestion: Break these into small pieces and sprinkle over ice cream. Makes a nice homemade topping.

Coconut-Sesame Refrigerator Cookies

A light cookie flavored with sesame seed, along with a hint of almond and coconut.

Preparation time: 25 minutes
Refrigerate: 3 hours

1	cup (2 sticks) butter or margarine, softened	¾	cup flaked coconut
¾	cups granulated sugar	¼	cup almonds, finely chopped
1½	cups all-purpose flour	¼	teaspoon almond extract
¾	cup sesame seeds, lightly toasted		Dash salt

Cream the butter in a large bowl. Gradually add the sugar, beating until fluffy. Mix in the flour until well-blended.

Stir in all of the remaining ingredients.

Divide dough into thirds. Roll into 2″ × 12″ logs and wrap tightly with waxed paper or plastic wrap. Refrigerate 3 hours or freeze.

Final preparation time: 5 minutes
Pan: cookie sheet, ungreased
Oven: 300°F. for 30 minutes
Yield: 30 cookies

When ready to bake, preheat oven to 300°F.

Cut logs into slices about ¼-inch thick. Bake on ungreased cookie sheets for 30 minutes. Remove lightly browned cookies to wire rack to cool. Freeze well but be sure to layer with waxed paper.

Mincemeat Refrigerator Cookies

Here's an easy refrigerator cookie that captures the pungent flavor of mincemeat. Serve these with rice pudding, vanilla custard or ice cream.

Preparation time: 40 minutes   **Refrigerate:** 3 hours or overnight

¾	cup butter	¾	cup prepared mincemeat
1	cup granulated sugar	3	cups flour, sifted
1	egg	½	teaspoon baking soda
½	teaspoon vanilla extract	½	teaspoon salt
1	teaspoon grated lemon peel	1	teaspoon ground cinnamon
		¾	cup nuts, chopped

In a large bowl, cream together the butter and sugar, until fluffy. Beat in the egg, vanilla extract and lemon peel. Stir in the mincemeat and set aside.

Sift the flour, baking soda, salt and cinnamon together. Gradually add the sifted dry ingredients to the creamed mixture. Mix well. Stir in the nuts.

Divide the dough in half. Place each half on a sheet of waxed paper and roll to about 12 inches long. Wrap rolls in the waxed paper, and refrigerate several hours or as long as 2 to 3 days.

Final preparation time: 5 minutes   **Oven:** 375°F. for 10 minutes
Pan: cookie sheets, ungreased   **Yield:** 100 cookies

When ready to bake, preheat oven to 375°F.

Slice rolls into ⅛-inch slices and place on ungreased cookie sheets, about 2 inches apart. Bake for 10 minutes. Remove cookies to wire racks to cool.

Syl's Yeast Rugelah

The rich filling with a hint of almond puts these cookies into a class of their own! This is a very impressive cookie – always popular – and its crescent shape adds interest to any platter of cookies.

Preparation time: 20 minutes
Refrigerate: 3 hours

Pastry:

½   cup sour cream
1   tablespoon boiling water
1   package (¼ oz.) dry yeast
1   cup butter or margarine, softened

¾   cup all-purpose flour, sifted
2   egg yolks (reserve the whites for filling)
1¾ cups all-purpose flour, sifted

In a small bowl, sprinkle yeast on water, and stir until dissolved. Add sour cream, and mix. Let stand for 3 minutes.

Place softened butter and ½ cup flour in a large bowl. Add sour cream mixture and beat all together for 1 minute at low speed.

Add egg yolks, and an additional ¼ cup flour. Beat for 1 minute at medium speed. Stir in the remaining 1¾ cups flour until a soft dough forms.

Turn dough onto a floured board and knead for 8 to 10 minutes. Divide into 6 balls, and refrigerate for 3 hours (or up to 5 days).

Final preparation time: 1 hour
Pan: cookie sheet, ungreased
Oven: 375°F. for 15 to 20 minutes
Yield: 48 crescent cookies

Filling:

1 cup almonds (or other nuts), chopped	1 teaspoon vanilla extract
½ cup granulated sugar	1 teaspoon almond extract
	2 egg whites, stiffly beaten

When ready to bake, preheat oven to 375°F.

In a medium bowl, combine the filling ingredients, folding in the stiffly beaten egg whites last.

Roll as in *Cinnamon Crescents* (page 114) placing filling on top of dough only.

Let stand 15 minutes before baking. Bake on ungreased cookie sheet for 20 minutes or until golden. Remove cookies to cool on wire rack. These freeze very well.

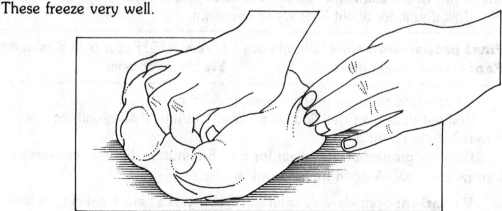

Kneading the Rugelah Dough

Jasper Sour Cream Cookies

This is a good cookie-cutter recipe, which I have been baking for over 40 years now.

Preparation time: 15 minutes   **Refrigerate:** 3 hours

4 cups all-purpose flour	2 eggs
1 teaspoon baking soda	1 cup sour cream
1 teaspoon baking powder	1 teaspoon vanilla extract
1 cup vegetable shortening	1 cup chopped dates or raisins
1¾ cups granulated sugar	
½ teaspoon salt	

In a large bowl, sift together flour, baking soda, and baking powder. Set aside.

In a large bowl, cream together the shortening and sugar. Mix in the salt and eggs. Add the sour cream and sifted dry ingredients alternately. Mix in the vanilla extract, and lastly the dates and raisins.

Chill dough for about 3 hours or overnight.

Final preparation time: 35 minutes   **Oven:** 425°F. for 6 to 8 minutes
Pan: cookie sheets, greased   **Yield:** 96 cookies

When ready to bake, preheat oven to 425°F.

Roll out dough on well-floured surface. Cut into shapes with cookie cutters, or the rim of a glass.

Bake on greased cookie sheet for 6 to 8 minutes. Remove cookies to wire rack to cool. A good freezer cookie.

Variation: Sprinkle with colored sugar crystals before baking, or frost with *No-Fuss Cookie Frosting*.

No-Fuss Cookie Frosting

Most cookies don't need a frosting; they taste better and look inviting without a frosted surface. But sometimes – especially for holidays or birthday parties – you want that extra hint of sweetness and color. Here's the perfect frosting.

Preparation time: 15 minutes

1 cup powdered sugar, sifted	1½ tablespoons cream
¼ teaspoon salt	3 drops food coloring (optional)
½ teaspoon vanilla extract (or other flavoring, such as almond or mint)	Grated orange or lemon rind (optional)

Blend all ingredients until smooth, adding just enough cream to spread easily.

Spread on cookies with small spatula. Decorate with colored sugar crystals or chocolate sprinkles if desired.

Note: This frosting works well on *Sugar Cookies, Honey Raisin Cookies, Orange-Sour Cream Cut-Out Cookies, Jasper Sour Cream Cookies* and *Butter Delights.*

Orange-Sour Cream Cut-Out Cookies

Make this batter the night before you plan to bake these very rich cookies. This is a good one to bake with kids using cookie cutters. Frost when cool.

Preparation time: 30 minutes
Refrigerate: overnight

1 cup butter or margarine, softened
1¼ cups granulated sugar
2 eggs
3¼ cups all-purpose flour

1 teaspoon baking powder
1 cup sour cream
Grated rind of 1 orange (about 2 teaspoons)

In a large bowl, cream the butter and 1¼ cups granulated sugar together.

Add the eggs one at a time, beating thoroughly after each addition.

Sift flour and baking powder together. Alternating with the sour cream, add flour mixture to the creamed mixture. Blend very well and add orange rind.

Wrap tightly and chill overnight.

Final preparation time: 50 minutes
Pan: cookie sheet, greased
Oven: 375°F. for 12 minutes
Yield: 96 cookies

Topping:

⅓ cup granulated sugar

⅓ cup almonds, finely chopped

Preheat oven to 375°F.

Turn dough out on floured board, and roll or press to ¼-inch thickness. Cut cookies with cookie cutters, or the rim of a 2-inch wide glass.

Combine the chopped almonds and sugar; sprinkle on cookies.

Bake on greased baking sheet for 10 to 12 minutes. Remove cookies to wire rack to cool.

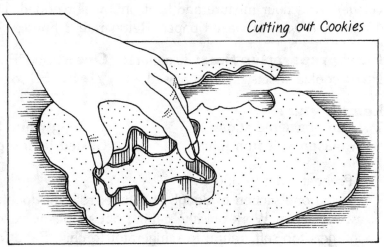

Cutting out Cookies

Kids Cut-Outs

These are fun to make with children. I prepare the dough in the morning, and then when my grandchildren arrive, we set about the task of cutting our shapes, baking, glazing . . . and licking the bowl!

Preparation time: 25 minutes   **Refrigerate:** 2 hours

5	cups all-purpose flour	1	cup (2 sticks) butter or margarine, softened
1½	teaspoons baking soda		
½	teaspoon salt	1	cup granulated sugar
2	teaspoons ginger	1	egg
1	teaspoon cinnamon	1	cup molasses
1	teaspoon ground cloves	2	tablespoons vinegar

Sift together flour, baking soda, salt and 3 spices. In large bowl, beat butter, adding sugar until light and fluffy. Beat in egg, molasses and vinegar. Add flour mixture and beat until well blended. Divide dough into 4 parts and wrap in waxed paper. Refrigerate 2 hours.

Final preparation time: 30 minutes   **Oven:** 350°F., 8–10 minutes
Pan: cookie sheets, lightly greased   **Yield:** 50 cookies

Lemon glaze:

1	cup powdered sugar	1	egg white
⅛–¼	teaspoon lemon juice		Grated lemon peel

Preheat oven to 350°F.

Using one section of dough at a time, roll out dough between sheets of waxed paper. Work quickly, cutting out shapes with cookie cutters. If dough gets too soft, return to refrigerator to chill. Bake for 8–10 minutes. Mix together lemon glaze ingredients. Remove cookies from oven and glaze lightly while still hot. Cool on wire rack.

Grandma's Brown Lace Cookies

Absolutely delicious! These are almost unbeatable – a dessert in themselves served with tea, coffee, or milk.

Preparation time: 25 minutes
Refrigerate: 1 hour or overnight

¼	cup (4 tablespoons) butter or margarine	½	cup all-purpose flour
2	cups brown sugar, packed	1	teaspoon baking powder
2	eggs, well-beaten	1	cup pecans, coarsely chopped
1	teaspoon vanilla extract		

In a medium bowl, cream the butter and brown sugar. Add the beaten eggs, and beat all together until well-blended. Add the vanilla extract and mix.

Sift flour and baking powder together. Mix in the chopped nuts.

Gradually add the flour mixture to the creamed ingredients. Mix until well-blended. Cover with waxed paper and refrigerate at least one hour.

Final preparation time: 10 minutes
Pans: cookie sheets, greased and floured
Oven: 400°F. for 6 to 8 minutes
Yield: 30 cookies

When ready to bake, preheat oven to 400°F.

Remove dough from refrigerator. Grease cookie sheets and then sprinkle with flour. Drop dough by ½ teaspoonfuls, about 3 inches apart onto cookie sheets. Bake for 6 to 8 minutes.

Remove from pan when *slightly* cooled, to wire racks.

These are very delicate so freeze carefully.

Pineapple Drops

This cookie has a cake-like texture and is not too sweet. A nice cookie for mid-morning snack at school, office, or home.

Preparation time: 20 to 25 minutes
Refrigerate: at least 1 hour

1	cup vegetable shortening	3½	cups all-purpose flour, sifted
2	cups granulated sugar	1	teaspoon baking soda
1	egg	½	teaspoon salt
1	can (8 oz.) crushed pineapple with liquid	¼	teaspoon ground nutmeg
		½	cup nuts, chopped

In a large bowl, beat together shortening, sugar and egg. Mix in the pineapple with liquid.

Sift the flour, baking soda, salt, and nutmeg together. Add to creamed mixture. Stir in nuts.

Chill batter at least 1 hour.

Final preparation time: 10 minutes
Pan: cookie sheets, greased
Oven: 400°F. for 8 to 10 minutes
Yield: 72 cookies

When ready to bake, preheat oven to 400°F.

Drop batter by teaspoonfuls on greased cookie sheet. Bake for 8 to 10 minutes or until no imprint remains when touched lightly.

Remove cookies to wire rack to cool. These freeze well.

Variation: For a sweeter cookie, sprinkle with sifted powdered sugar while still warm.

Ginger Snaps

Sprinkle 2 to 3 drops of water on unbaked cookies to get that traditional crinkled ginger snap surface.

Preparation time: 15 minutes | **Refrigerate:** ½ hour

¾	cup vegetable shortening	2	cups all-purpose flour
1	cup granulated sugar	1	teaspoon baking soda
1	egg	1	teaspoon ground cinnamon
¼	cup molasses	1	teaspoon ground cloves
		1	teaspoon ground ginger

In a large bowl, cream together the butter, sugar, egg and molasses until well-blended.

Sift the flour, baking soda and spices together. Add to the creamed mixture. Mix until thoroughly blended.

Wrap and refrigerate dough for ½ hour.

Final preparation time: 10 minutes
Pan: cookie sheets, greased
Oven: 375°F. for 10 to 12 minutes
Yield: 84 cookies

Topping:
⅓ cup granulated sugar

When ready to bake, preheat oven to 375°F.

In your hands, roll dough into balls about half-teaspoon size. Dip each ball into sugar topping. Place on greased cookie sheet about 2-inches apart. Sprinkle 2 to 3 drops of water on each cookie. Bake for 10 to 12 minutes. Remove dark brown cookies to cool on wire rack. These freeze very well.

5

Golde's Fun and Festive Cookies

A variety of cookies – some molded, some shaped, some simply formed into a ball – but all quite simple to bake, and pretty to look at. Many of these recipes are perfect for baking with children.

BAKING WITH CHILDREN

Kids – both boys and girls – have a wonderful time baking. It's one of those activities where grown-ups, young children, and teenagers can all share in a creative effort, and then delight in the outcome. Baking with children can be as creative as you like, as personal as you want, humorous or serious, precise or not – whatever environment you create.

Depending on the age of the children, you may want to have the batter partially prepared. Older children, though, will want to make the batter from scratch. Some children may only need to stir a few times before shaping the batter; little ones may be thrilled to pick and choose garnishes for already formed cookies (try *Jewel's Cookies* for the youngest ones). Use your judgment as to what your particular group is capable of doing, and prepare everything up to that point *before* they join you.

TEACHING WHILE YOU BAKE

It's never too early (or too late, for that matter) to teach children the rudiments of good baking. I used to teach the local Girl Scout troops their Baking Badge, and years later some of the, now grown, women stop by to say they still follow my instructions.
- Emphasize reading the recipe before you start.
- Assemble all ingredients and explain what they are used for, such as baking soda as a leavening.
- Demonstrate how to properly measure liquids (in a glass measuring cup, on a flat surface) and dry ingredients (in graduated measuring cups, levelled with a knife).

- Stress to never measure over the batter bowl in case of a spill.
- Teach the children all about eggs. How to crack them and how to separate them (again not over the batter bowl). How to mix them slightly or beat them to a yellow foam. How to beat egg whites and *fold* them in.
- Encourage children to get "into" the cookie-making process. Try to avoid fussing about spills, but rather encourage their natural spontaneity and clever ideas. Your kitchen will be chaotic, but the positive baking experience will last for many, many years.
- If possible, choose a recipe that has fun built into it.
  Provide a wide assortment of cookie cutters, garnishes,
  colored sugar crystals, fillings, and let their imaginations run wild.
  You'll be amazed at what they think of – some cookies will be
  loaded down with everything, others well be sparsely decorated.
- Teach subtly and quietly, more by example than by correcting what they do. Keep conversation flowing, asking what they are making, gently explaining what you are doing. Give lots of praise and encouragement.
- Assign everyone a small clean-up task, so that, too, becomes part of the overall experience.
- Share the fruits of their labor, both by admiring the freshly baked cookies, eating some all together, and giving everyone a few to take home.
- Most importantly, really enjoy the time you spend baking with children. Listen to what they say, acknowledge their ideas and cookie creations. They'll respond so warmly that you'll be smiling for a long time to come. It really is a special time together.

Poppy Seed-Lemon Cookies

You can either make these with a cookie press in interesting shapes, cut with cookie cutters, or simply roll them. Either way, these are delicate cookies with the subtle flavors of poppy seeds and lemon.

Preparation time: 25 minutes
Pan: cookie sheet, greased
Oven: 400°F. for 8 to 10 minutes
Yield: 50 cookies

½	cup (1 stick) butter or margarine, softened	⅓	cup poppy seeds
½	cup granulated sugar	1½	cups all-purpose flour
1	egg, beaten	1	teaspoon lemon juice
1	teaspoon baking powder	½	teaspoon lemon rind, grated
¼	teaspoon salt		

Preheat oven to 400°F.

In a large bowl, cream the butter and sugar together. Add the beaten egg and mix well. Set aside.

Sift the flour, baking powder and salt together.

Gradually add the flour to the creamed mixture and blend well. Add the poppy seeds. Flavor with lemon juice and rind.

If using cookie press, fill and press onto greased cookie sheet. Or roll out dough on floured board until quite thin, and cut with cookie cutters or with the rim of a 2-inch glass.

Bake for 8 to 10 minutes. Remove cookies and cool on wire racks.

Jewel's Cookies

My grandchildren always ask to bake these with me – it's a perfect recipe to use with children!

Preparation time: 20 minutes
Pan: cookie sheet, lightly greased
Oven: 350°F. for 25 minutes
Yield: 36 cookies

Pastry:
2   cups all-purpose flour
1   cup (2 sticks) butter or margarine, softened
½   cup granulated sugar
2   egg yolks

Filling:
1   jar of jam or preserves, maraschino cherries, glazed fruit, nuts, or chocolate kisses

Preheat oven to 350°F.

In a large bowl, mix all of the pastry ingredients together until well-blended.

Break off walnut-sized pieces of dough and roll into balls. Flatten each ball in its center with your thumb and fill with whatever you choose – jams and cherries look pretty. A variety of fillings make an attractive assortment.

Bake on lightly greased cookie sheets for 25 minutes. Remove cookies to wire rack to cool.

Variation: This cookie is an ideal choice if you want to tint some cookies a pale pink. Just add 2 to 3 drops of red food coloring to batter.

Molasses 'n Spice Cookies

A rich, dark, spicy cookie that is especially nice to serve in the deep winter months.

Preparation time: 25 minutes
Pan: cookie sheet, ungreased
Oven: 375°F. for 10 minutes
Yield: 60 cookies

2	cups all-purpose flour	1	cup granulated sugar
1	teaspoon baking soda	¼	teaspoon salt
1	teaspoon ground ginger	1	egg, beaten
1	teaspoon ground cloves	¼	cup molasses
1	teaspoon ground cinnamon		
¾	cups vegetable shortening, melted		

Preheat oven to 375°F.

Sift the flour, baking soda and spices together. Set aside.

In a large bowl, cool melted shortening. Add sugar, salt, egg and molasses. Then, add sifted ingredients. Mix until well-blended.

Form walnut-sized balls, place on ungreased cookie sheets, and press flat with back of fork.

Bake for 10 minutes. Remove cookies to wire racks to cool.

Butter Delights

These are almost as light and buttery as shortbread cookies, and much easier to make!

Preparation time: 15 minutes
Pan: cookie sheet, greased
Oven: 375°F. for 15 minutes
Yield: 36 cookies

1½ cups all-purpose flour, sifted
½ cup cornstarch

½ cup granulated sugar
1 cup (2 sticks) sweet butter or margarine, softened

Preheat oven to 375°F.

In a medium bowl, mix all ingredients together until well-blended.

Break off walnut-sized pieces. Roll into balls and flatten each with the back of a fork (so fork lines show).

Bake on a greased cookie sheet for 13 to 15 minutes or until lightly browned. Remove cookies to wire rack to cool.

Variation: If you have small butter molds, try pressing these against cookies to create interesting designs.

Variation: *Butter Delights* are perfect for adding a drop or two of red or green food coloring to final batter. Sprinkle with red or green sugar crystals when almost cool or roll balls in sugar crystals before baking.

Confetti Date Balls

These are a visual treat, as well as a rich-tasting confection. Perfect for gift tins, as well as in small candy dishes.

Preparation time: 20 minutes
Pan: cookie sheet, greased
Oven: 350°F. for 12 to 15 minutes
Yield: 36 cookies

1	(8 oz.) package dates	1	cup brown sugar, firmly packed
1	teaspoon water		
1	tablespoon butter	2	egg whites, beaten stiff
1	cup walnuts, coarsely chopped	1	cup shredded coconut

Preheat oven to 350°F.

In a small saucepan, soften the dates in the butter, along with about 1 teaspoon of water. Cook over very low heat, and watch carefully, stirring to prevent scorching (or soften in double boiler).

In a medium bowl, combine softened dates with the brown sugar and chopped nuts. Fold in the stiffly beaten egg whites.

Form into walnut-sized balls, and roll each ball in the coconut. Bake on greased cookie sheets for 12 to 15 minutes, until lightly browned.

Cool date balls on wire rack. These freeze very well.

Chocolate Crackles

Enjoy these luscious chocolate treats . . . and try not to eat them all at one sitting!

Preparation time: 35 minutes
Pan: cookie sheet, lined with foil

Oven: 350°F. for 12 to 14 minutes
Yield: 96 cookies

3 cups all-purpose flour	2 tablespoons water
1¼ teaspoons baking soda	2 cups (12 oz.) semisweet chocolate pieces
½ teaspoon salt	
1½ cups dark brown sugar, packed	2 eggs
¾ cups butter or margarine, softened	½ cup granulated sugar (optional)

Preheat oven to 350°F.

Sift the flour, baking soda, and salt together. Set aside.

In a large saucepan, cook the butter, brown sugar and water, stirring until the butter melts. Add the chocolate pieces, stirring until the chocolate is almost melted. Remove from heat and stir until chocolate is completely melted. Transfer chocolate mixture to a large bowl and let cool slightly (5 minutes).

Beat eggs one at a time into chocolate mixture with electric mixer on high speed. Reduce speed, and gradually add sifted dry ingredients. Let batter set until dough can be handled (about 10 minutes; don't refrigerate).

Line a cookie sheet with aluminum foil. Roll dough into walnut-sized balls, about 20 balls to a cookie sheet. You can roll each ball in granulated sugar before baking, if you choose.

Bake for 12 to 14 minutes. Tops will feel dry, but not firm. The cookies will crisp as they cool on wire racks. These freeze very well.

Shortbread Logs

Rolled shortbread with a touch of chocolate – what could be better? These look especially nice on a platter of fancy cookies.

Preparation time: 35 minutes
Pan: cookie sheets, ungreased
Oven: 350°F. for 12–13 minutes
Yield: 72 cookies

Cookie Dough:
1   cup (2 sticks) butter or margarine, softened
2   cups flour
½   cup powdered sugar, sifted
1   teaspoon vanilla extract

Frosting:
1   cup (6 ounces) semisweet chocolate pieces
1   tablespoon butter
½   cup pecans, finely chopped

Preheat oven to 350°F.

In a large bowl, cream butter. Add powdered sugar, flour and vanilla. Beat well. Using 1 teaspoon of dough, shape into individual 2″ logs. Bake for 12–13 minutes. Remove from cookie sheet and cool on wire rack.

While cookies cool, melt chocolate and butter in the microwave or double boiler. Stir. (Add 1 tablespoon milk if too thick for dipping.)

Dip ½ of each cookie (½ chocolate covered, ½ plain) or both ends into chocolate. Then dip into nuts. Place on cookie sheets lined with waxed-paper and refrigerate until chocolate is firm, about 1 hour.

Butterscotch Cookies

These are cake-like in texture with a rich brown sugar frosting.

Preparation time: 40 minutes
Pan: cookie sheets, greased

Oven: 350°F. for 10 minutes
Yield: 60 cookies

Dough:
1   tablespoon vinegar
1   cup evaporated milk
½   cup (1 stick) margarine or butter, softened
1½ cups brown sugar, firmly packed
2   eggs
1   teaspoon vanilla extract
2½ cups flour, sifted

1   teaspoon baking soda
½   teaspoon baking powder
½   teaspoon salt
⅔   cup nuts, chopped

Frosting:
½   cup (1 stick) butter or margarine
2   cups powdered sugar, sifted
2–4 tablespoons water, boiling
Walnut or pecan halves

Preheat oven to 350°F.

Pour vinegar in a 1-cup measure. Add the evaporated milk and set aside. In a large bowl, beat the butter until light. Add the brown sugar and continue beating. Add eggs and vanilla, beating until well blended.

Sift the flour, baking soda, baking powder and salt together. Stir evaporated milk. Alternately add milk and dry ingredients to creamed mixture. Mix in chopped nuts. Drop by rounded tablespoonfuls onto cookie sheets about 2½″ apart. Bake for 10–12 minutes, until lightly browned and almost firm to touch.

To prepare frosting, melt butter, stirring constantly over medium heat until butter stops bubbling and is medium brown. Combine with powdered sugar, and 2 to 4 tablespoons boiling water. Beat until smooth, and of spreading consistency. Frost cooled cookies and top with nut half.

Golden Nuggets

These are a favorite cookie because they are so versatile – fill them with whatever you have on hand, or roll them in colorful sugar crystals.

Preparation time: 25 minutes
Pan: cookie sheet, greased

Oven: 325°F. for 25 to 30 minutes
Yield: 36 cookies

1 cup (2 sticks) butter or margarine, softened
½ cup granulated sugar
1 egg yolk, unbeaten
1 teaspoon grated orange rind
2½ cups all-purpose flour, sifted

Filling:
Dates, nuts, jam, maraschino cherries, chocolate pieces, or any other filling of your choice
Powdered sugar, sifted

Preheat oven to 325°F.

In a large bowl, cream together the butter and sugar. Add the egg yolk and rind, blending well.

Mix in the flour, forming a heavy dough.

Take a walnut-sized piece of dough and flatten in your hand. Fill center with filling of your choice, and shape dough around it; roll into a ball. Place on greased cookie sheet, and bake 25 to 30 minutes. Nuggets will be quite light in color even when they are done.

Remove nuggets to wire rack, and sprinkle with powdered sugar while still hot.

These freeze well, but wait to sprinkle with powdered sugar after defrosting.

Variation: For special treats, add 1 or 2 drops (no more) of pink food coloring to the dough. They look very festive with the powdered sugar. Or before baking, roll in colorful crystals, confetti sprinkles, or cinnamon sugar.

No-Bake Rum Balls

A no-bake confection that can be served as you would chocolate truffles with after-dinner coffee.

Preparation time: 15 minutes
Pan: store in covered tin
Oven: no baking
Yield: 36 balls

2½ cups vanilla wafers, crushed	1 cup walnuts, chopped
2 tablespoons cocoa	3 tablespoons dark corn syrup
1 cup powdered sugar	¼ cup rum (or brandy)

In a medium bowl, mix all ingredients together in the order listed.

When well-blended, form into walnut-sized balls. Roll balls in additional powdered sugar.

Store in covered tin.

Mocha Nut Cookies

A mild flavored tea cookie that's not too sweet. A nice late-evening snack with tea or milk.

Preparation time: 25 minutes
Pan: cookie sheet, greased
Oven: 325°F. for 13 to 15 minutes
Yield: 48 cookies

1 cup butter or margarine, softened	1¾ cups all-purpose flour, sifted
½ cup granulated sugar	½ teaspoon salt
2 teaspoons vanilla extract	2 cups nuts, finely chopped
1 egg yolk	⅓ cup powdered sugar
¼ cup cocoa	

Preheat oven to 325°F.

In a large bowl, cream together the butter, sugar, and vanilla. When well-blended, add the egg yolk and mix.

Sift together the cocoa, flour, and salt. Add the creamed mixture. Mix batter well. Add the nuts.

Shape dough into walnut-sized balls, and place on a greased cookie sheet. Bake for 13 to 15 minutes. Remove to a wire rack. Roll in powdered sugar when almost cool.

Variation: Substitute 1½ cups shredded coconut for chopped nuts.

Pecan Butter Balls

Wonderfully simple . . . simply wonderful!

Preparation time: 20 minutes
Pan: cookie sheets, greased
Oven: 300°F. for 30 minutes
Yield: 30 cookies

½	cup butter or margarine, softened	
2	tablespoons sugar	
1	teaspoon vanilla extract	

1   cup pecans, finely chopped
1   cup all-purpose flour, sifted
Powdered sugar

Preheat oven to 300°F.

Beat the butter until creamy. Add the sugar and vanilla extract, and continue to beat well. Stir in the chopped pecans and sifted flour.

Roll small pieces of dough into small balls, and bake for 30 minutes.

While still hot, roll balls in powdered sugar.

Return to oven for 1 minute so cookies will form glaze.

Remove to wire rack to cool.

These freeze very well.

Pecan Fingers

Sweet, chewy, and attractive, with the added bonus of being very easy to make, too!

Preparation time: 20 minutes
Pan: cookie sheets, greased
Oven: 325°F. for 25 to 30 minutes
Yield: 48 cookies

1 cup butter	1½ cups pecans, coarsely chopped
¾ cup powdered sugar	1 tablespoon ice water
1 teaspoon vanilla extract	⅛ teaspoon salt
2 cups flour, sifted	Powdered sugar

Preheat oven to 325°F.

In a medium bowl, cream the butter and powdered sugar together. Add the remaining ingredients, and mix well.

Break off small pieces of dough and roll with palm of hands into finger lengths.

Bake for 25 to 30 minutes. Remove from oven to cool on wire racks. While still slightly warm, roll each cookie in additional powdered sugar.

These freeze well. They look freshest when rolled in powdered sugar after defrosting. (Heat slightly in oven before rolling.)

CHAPTER

6

Golde's Specialty Cookies

Many of the recipes in this chapter are personal favorites of mine, but that is not the reason I included them here. These cookies add visual appeal to any assortment of cookies, whether served at home or packaged for a gift. And visual appeal is well worth considering in any cookie presentation.

Sometimes of course, there is nothing better than a plate piled high with one kind of cookie. Certainly *Chocolate Chip Crispers* or *Zucchini Oatmeal Cookies* can be consumed in large quantities faster than you can pour milk for a cookies 'n milk snack. At other times a more varied presentation will be effective in creating the atmosphere you want.

PRESENTATION POINTERS

- Select cookies appropriate to the occasion and setting. Will the people be sitting or standing? Some cookies are more difficult to eat without a napkin or plate.
- How do you want your platter to look – casual with cookies heaped on, or formally arranged with each cookie having a place of its own?
- For large platters, arrange all cookies of one kind together, rather than mixing them throughout. This way you achieve visual appeal, as well as avoid a mingling of flavors. Each type of cookie can make a statement.
- Will the cookies be the main dessert or are they an adjunct to another dessert?
- Select an appropriately-sized platter, tray or dish to serve your cookies on. If it looks over-crowded or too sparsely covered, people are reluctant to help themselves.

- Try using several small, unusually shaped, silver serving dishes, each with a single kind of attractive cookie, such as a small dish of *Cinnamon Crescents*, another of *Cream Puff Pastries with Strawberry Filling*, and a third dish of *Walnut Surprises*. Pass these around the dining table when coffee is served.
- Consider unusual dishes for presenting your cookies. Baskets lined with linen napkins are very festive; odd pieces of china, pottery or crystal make interesting serving pieces, as well as beautifully polished silver trays and pewter platters.
- Keep cookies well covered until ready to serve to prevent drying out.
- Refresh frozen cookies with a sprinkling of sifted powdered sugar.

COOKIES AND . . .

It's good to stretch your imagination when it comes to serving ideas. Cookies and milk go together as well as peanut butter and jelly, but there are many other pleasing combinations.

- Serve cookies with fresh fruit cup. Just before serving, add a generous sprinkling of champagne to your fresh fruit mixture. Pass a plate of *Lemon Squares* and *Raisin Nut Tarts*.
- Try strawberries and cream with a platter of *Accordion Treats*.
- Pass a dessert cheese such as Kirsch Gourmandaise along with bunches of green and red grapes. Place a platter of *Coconut-Sesame Cookies* and *Lemony Pecan Bars* on the table's center.
- Serve a dessert coffee along with a platter of *Seafoam Chews* and *Cream Cheese Tarts*.

- Serve hot baked apples. Pass bowls of honey, whipped cream and a basket of *Spicy Fruit Cookies*.
- Try coffee ice cream topped with warm maple syrup. Pass the *Double Fudge Brownies Supreme*.
- You'll delight in homemade raspberry sherbet along with wonderful *Chinese Chews*.
- Scoop some vanilla ice cream on top of generous portions of *Pecan Pie Treasures*.
- Whenever you serve custards, puddings or souffles, place a few small dishes of cookies on the table to munch while lingering over coffee. Try *Crispy Oatmeal-Raisin Cookies, or Pecan Butter Balls*.
- Serving a heavy dessert? Pass some light cookies such as *Chocolate Thinsees, Butter Delights*, and *Poppy-Seed Lemon Cookies*.
- Serve your favorite ice cream in champagne glasses. Cover with a splash of Kahlua or Amaretto Liqueur, and crumble *Oriental Crunch* on top.

As you can see, cookies complement just about any dessert. An attractive presentation enhances your table and creates a welcoming environment.

And it's amazing how quickly a group can relax around a plate of aromatic delicious cookies. "Cookie comraderie" is a great icebreaker. Somehow cookies and friendliness go together. I tend to think that is because homebaked cookies used to say "I care about you" to us as children, and so, they still communicate affection to us as adults.

Here's to broadening your cookie experience!

Bev's Shortbread Cookies

This is a very special cookie – so rich and buttery that it seems to melt in your mouth. I always baked these with my daughters for all our neighbors at holiday time.

Preparation time: 25 minutes
Pan: cookie sheet, greased
Oven: 375°F. for 8 to 10 minutes
Yield: 70 small cookies

1 cup (2 sticks) butter, softened	½ teaspoon vanilla extract
½ cup powdered sugar	Pinch salt
2 cups all-purpose flour, sifted	2 to 3 drops red or green food coloring (optional)
	Decorative edibles (optional)

Note: This cookie can only be made with a cookie press, as they don't roll out nicely.

Preheat oven to 375°F.

In a medium bowl, cream all ingredients together until very well-blended. (Use your food processor, if you have one).

Fill cookie press, and squeeze cookies out onto greased cookie sheet. Use a variety of shapes and designs.

Bake for 8 to 10 minutes. Cookies will be very pale, slightly browned at bottom, when done. Remove cookies to wire rack to cool and decorate.

These make a wonderful tea cookie, and they freeze very well.

Variations: For colorful cookies, tint batter. Press out into varied designs. Decorate with cherries, chips and jams before baking. Decorate with sugar crystals, chocolate sprinkles or confetti sprinkles after baking, but before completely cooled.

Gingery Almond Crisps

A perfectly delightful dessert!

Preparation time: 30–45 minutes
Pan: cookie sheets, lined with foil, greased and floured
Oven: 350°F. for 17–18 minutes
Yield: 20 large, 10 colossal

1	cup blanched almonds, toasted	½	teaspoon salt
1	piece fresh ginger (4″), peeled and diced	½	cup unsalted butter, softened
1½	cups all-purpose flour, sifted	¾	cup granulated sugar
¼	cup (1 ounce) crystallized ginger, minced	1	egg, beaten
1	teaspoon ground ginger	1	teaspoon almond extract
		⅛	teaspoon salt

Preheat oven to 350°F.

Coarsely chop ½ cup almonds. Over small bowl, press diced fresh ginger through a garlic press to extract juices. Set aside.

In a medium bowl, combine chopped almonds, flour, crystallized ginger, ground ginger and ½ teaspoon salt. In a larger bowl, cream butter until light. Add sugar and beat until fluffy. Blend in ¼ teaspoon pressed ginger juice, 1 tablespoon of beaten egg (reserve remainder) and almond extract. Add flour mixture and blend well. Gather dough into ball.

Break off 1 heaping tablespoon at a time and form into balls. Set on cookie sheet and flatten into 2½″ rounds. Mix remaining egg with ⅛ teaspoon salt. Lightly brush cookies with egg. Press remaining almonds on each cookie, arranging from center like spokes of a wheel. Brush almonds with egg glaze. Bake for 10 minutes. Reverse sheets and bake an additional 7–8 minutes. When golden brown, cool on wire rack.

Open Sesames

This is a very rich cookie, with a wonderful sesame crunch. If the ingredient halvah (a sesame and honey confection) is unfamiliar to you, just ask for it at the supermarket.

Preparation time: 45 minutes
Pan: cookie sheets, lined with foil

Oven: 325°F. for 20 minutes
Yield: 36 cookies

2½ cups all-purpose flour, sifted	1 large egg
1¾ cups powdered sugar	4 teaspoons fresh lemon juice
¾ teaspoon salt	1 tablespoon vanilla
¼ teaspoon baking powder	1½ teaspoons grated lemon peel
½ cup (1 stick) unsalted butter, cut in pieces	½ teaspoon dark rum (or flavoring)
¾ cup (about 3–4 ounces) vanilla halvah, diced	¼ teaspoon oriental sesame oil
1¼ cups sesame seeds, toasted	

Preheat oven to 325°F.

Blend together flour, sugar, salt and baking powder. Cut in butter and halvah until mixture is coarse and grainy. Mix in ¼ cup sesame seeds. In a small bowl, blend together egg, lemon juice, vanilla, lemon peel, rum and sesame oil. Add to flour mixture. Mix with a fork until moist lumps form. Knead mixture until dough forms.

Sprinkle remaining 1 cup sesame seeds on work surface. Take heaping tablespoons of dough and roll each into a ball in your hands. Press into seeds, flattening slightly with palm of hand. Turn over and flatten to 2½" round. Bake for 20 minutes, turning cookie sheet in oven half way through baking. Cookies should be golden brown. Cool cookies on wire racks.

Accordion Treats

This special recipe makes wedge-shaped, long, slim cookies.
Very elegant and very delicious, too!

Preparation time: 40 minutes   **Oven:** 325°F. for 25 to 30 minutes
Pan: cookie sheet with aluminum foil   **Yield:** 60 cookies

1	yard heavy duty aluminum foil
¾	cup butter
¾	cup granulated sugar
2	eggs
1	teaspoon vanilla extract
¼	teaspoon salt
1¼	cups flour, sifted

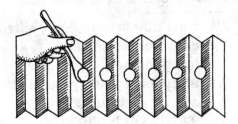

Preheat oven to 325°F.

To prepare foil accordion, fold 1 yard of foil lengthwise, to double thickness. Then, starting at top, fold into 1-inch accordion pleats. Pull open and place on cookie sheet or jelly-roll pan.

In large mixing bowl, cream butter. Gradually add the granulated sugar and cream very well, until light. Blend in eggs, vanilla extract and salt, and beat well. Gradually add sifted flour and mix thoroughly

Drop by *very* scant teaspoonfuls into center of folds of foil, one teaspoonful per fold. Use about one-half of the dough. The dough will spread in baking.

Bake for 25 to 30 minutes until pale golden. Remove pan to wire racks and cool for 10 minutes. Remove cookies from foil.

Shake off crumbs and reuse foil for remaining dough.

Chinese Chews

These are a family favorite – a chewy, sweet confection that goes with everything. The unusual rolled shape makes this visually appealing.

Preparation time: 15 minutes
Pan: 15" × 10" jelly-roll pan, greased
Oven: 350°F. for 20 to 25 minutes
Yield: 48 cookies

1 cup granulated sugar	1 cup walnuts, chopped
¾ cup all-purpose flour	2 eggs
¼ teaspoon salt	**Topping:**
1 teaspoon baking powder	½ cup sifted powdered sugar
1 cup dates, finely diced	

Preheat oven to 350°F.

In a large bowl, sift sugar, flour, salt, and baking powder together.

Add eggs, dates and nuts. Blend until a dough forms.

Pat the dough into a greased 15" × 10" jelly-roll pan.

Bake for 20 to 25 minutes.

Immediately upon removal from oven, cut into 1" × 1" squares, and roll crust side (top) inward in powdered sugar. The squares must still be warm enough to shape while rolling.

If they cool too much, return to the oven to warm.

Chinese Chews freeze very well.

Tart Pastry

Prepare your favorite 2-crust pie pastry for Raisin Nut Tarts and Butter Tarts, or use the following pastry recipe.

Preparation time: 10 minutes; refrigerate 2 hours.
Pan: tart tins
Yield: 2-crust pastry enough for 20 small tarts

1¾ cups all-purpose flour	¼ cup very cold water (approximate)
1 teaspoon salt	
⅔ cup vegetable shortening	

In a medium bowl, mix the flour and salt. Cut in the vegetable shortening until crumbly.

Add the water, little by little, until the dough can be gathered into a ball. It shouldn't be sticky so use as little water as possible.

Refrigerate dough for at least two hours.

When thoroughly chilled, roll dough out on floured surface. Cut pastry to fill bottom and sides of small paper tart cups. Fork holes into bottom dough. Follow tart recipes.

Rum Raisin Tarts

A dark brown sugar tart with a hint of rum and plenty of raisins and nuts.

Preparation time: 30 minutes
Pan: tart tins
Oven: 375°F. for 15 to 20 minutes
Yield: 20 small tarts

Prepare enough pie pastry for a 2-crust pie (page 126).
Press pastry into small paper tart cups along the bottom and sides.
Preheat oven to 375°F.

Filling:

1½ cups seedless raisins	2 cups brown sugar, packed
4 tablespoons butter	1 cup nuts, chopped
2 eggs	2 to 3 teaspoons rum

Soak the raisins in boiling water for a few minutes until softened. Strain and set raisins aside.

In a large bowl, beat the butter at medium speed until creamy. Add the eggs and brown sugar, and beat until foamy.

Mix in the rum, nuts, and raisins.

Fill unbaked tart crusts ⅔ full. Bake for 15 to 20 minutes until brown.

Remove from oven and cool tarts on wire rack.

Golden Butter Tarts

These are a delight. So light, yet also rich – that special butter-brown sugar balance.

Preparation time: 45 minutes
Pan: tart tins
Oven: 425°F. for 10 to 15 minutes
Yield: 20 small tarts

Prepare your favorite 2-crust pastry, or see page 126.
Preheat oven to 425°F.

Filling:

⅓ cup butter, melted
½ cup seedless raisins
½ cup golden corn syrup
½ cup brown sugar, packed
¼ teaspoon salt
1 egg

Melt the butter and set aside to cool. Beat egg.

In a medium bowl, mix together the melted butter and beaten egg. Add the brown sugar, salt, and syrup and continue mixing until smooth.

Line small tart cups with pastry along bottom and side. Fork holes in bottom.

Place 3 or 4 raisins in each tart cup, and spoon 1 scant teaspoon filling into each cup, leaving plenty of room for expansion.

Bake for 10 to 15 minutes on the lowest oven rack.

Remove from oven and let cool three minutes before removing from tins. Loosen edges of each tart with a knife, and continue cooling tarts on wire racks.

These freeze very well, although somewhat fragile.

Cream Cheese Tarts

If you like cheesecake, you'll love these small tarts. Smooth and creamy, they melt in your mouth. Best of all, they are easy to make and they freeze well, too.

Preparation time: 20 minutes
Pan: tart tins

Oven: 375°F. for 10 minutes
Yield: 24 small tarts

Crust:
1½ cups graham cracker crumbs
⅓ cup butter or margarine, melted

Filling:
1 lb. (16 oz.) cream cheese
2 eggs
1 teaspoon vanilla extract
½ cup granulated sugar

Preheat oven to 375°F.

Prepare crust by mixing graham cracker crumbs and melted butter together. Press about 1 tablespoon in each tart cup lined with tea papers. Set aside.

Prepare filling in a medium bowl by blending all filling ingredients together. Beat with an electric mixer for about 5 minutes.

Place a generous tablespoon of filling mixture on top of each crumb crust.

Bake for 10 minutes and remove from pan to cool on wire racks. Sprinkle a few graham cracker crumbs on top to give added color.

These freeze very well.

Variation 1: *Cinnamon Crust:* For just a hint of cinnamon in these tarts, add ¼ teaspoon ground cinnamon to crust ingredients.

Variation 2: *Raspberry Cheese Tarts:* Add ½ teaspoon of raspberry jam to each tart cup on top of crumb crust before filling with the cream cheese mixture.

Almond Brickles

My daughter, Debby, calls these "Dentist Delights." They look and taste very much like peanut brittle. These cookies take a little extra effort, but they are worth it.

Preparation time: 40 minutes
Pans: 15″ × 10″ jelly-roll pan, greased
Oven: 375°F. for 10 minutes (pastry);
          375°F. for 18 minutes (with topping)
Yield: 40 to 48 pieces

Pastry:
1¾   cups all-purpose flour
2½   tablespoons granulated sugar
¾   teaspoon baking powder
Dash salt
½   cup butter or margarine
1   egg, beaten
2   to 3 tablespoons milk or heavy cream

Preheat oven to 375°F.

Topping:
1½   cup granulated sugar
½   cup butter
½   cup heavy cream
¾   cup honey
1½   cups slivered almonds
¼   teaspoon vanilla extract

In a large bowl, thoroughly combine flour, 2½ tablespoons sugar, baking powder, and salt. Cut in ½ cup butter until mixture is crumbly. Then mix in the beaten egg. Add the milk gradually. Mix lightly until a light fluffy pastry forms. Gently pat into pan and bake at 375°F for 10 minutes.

Meanwhile, in a heavy saucepan prepare the topping by combining the sugar, butter, cream, vanilla extract, and honey. Cook over medium heat, stirring constantly. Test for doneness by dropping a small amount into cold water. When it comes out a firm but soft ball, it is ready. Pour topping over the baked pastry. Return to oven and bake 18 minutes until caramel colored. Sprinkle almonds evenly on top. Cut into squares while still warm and cool on wire rack. Or break into assorted pieces and cool. These freeze well but be sure to put waxed paper between layers.

Variation: Chopped peanuts are wonderful in this recipe, and less expensive than almonds. For baking, buy the generic unsalted peanuts which are lower priced and work just as well.

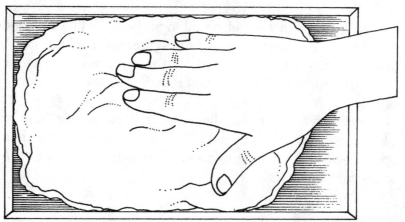

Patting Pastry into a jelly-roll pan

Brandy Snaps

These lacey, delicate cookies are perfect with light fruit desserts or dessert coffees; they are an elegant embellishment to any dessert. Try them too with a dish of coffee ice cream.

Preparation time: 15 minutes
Pan: cookie sheets, greased
Oven: 375°F. for 8 to 10 minutes
Yield: 100 cookies

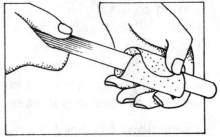

Shaping Brandy Snaps

1	cup brown sugar, packed
1	cup molasses
¾	cup butter, melted
2	teaspoons ground ginger
2	scant cups all-purpose flour, sifted

Preheat oven to 375°F.

In a large bowl, combine all ingredients until well-blended.

Drop by ½ teaspoonfuls onto a greased cookie sheet, leaving at least 3 inches between cookies, as these spread out quite a bit while baking.

Bake for 8 to 10 minutes, or until they are semi-crisp, lacey, and bubbly.

Remove from cookie sheet with a wide spatula, and immediately shape each cookie by rolling it, using the handle of a knife or handle of a wooden spoon before it has time to cool. Work quickly so that each can be shaped while still flexible.

These do not freeze well.

Pinwheel Pastries

A rich pastry, delicately folded into a pinwheel, filled with your favorite preserves. A very special cookie indeed!

*Preparation time: pastry: 15 minutes
wheels: 30 minutes
Pan: cookie sheet, lightly greased
Oven: 375°F. for 10 to 12 minutes
Yield: 48 pinwheels   *Pastry is refrigerated overnight

1 cup (2 sticks) butter, softened	2 cups flour, sifted
8 ounces (1 large package) cream cheese, softened	1 jar favorite preserves
	Walnuts, finely chopped (optional)

In a medium bowl, cream together butter and cream cheese. Add flour gradually and mix until very well-blended. Cover and refrigerate overnight.

Preheat oven to 375°F.

Roll out dough to about ⅛-inch thickness. Cut into rounds with rim of glass, about 2 inches in diameter. Place preserves (mixed with chopped nuts, if desired) in center of circle.

To shape into pinwheels, cut outer circle into fourths, leaving jam center intact. Fold ½ of each fourth over onto itself. Press folds down with top of fork.

Bake for 10 to 12 minutes until nicely browned. Remove pan from oven to cool for a minute or two, and then gently lift pinwheels off to cool on wire rack.

Variation: *Cheesey Pinwheel Pastries:* For a less sweet pastry, omit the jam filling. Instead sprinkle pastry circles with grated Parmesan Cheese. Fold into pinwheels and brush with beaten egg yolk; bake as above.

Cream Puff Pastries

*These are so versatile. Fill them with whatever you have on hand –
fresh fruit, whips, custards, ice cream, puddings – they always taste
delicious and look elegant.*

Preparation time: 25 minutes
Pan: cookie sheet, greased
Oven: 400°F. for 35 minutes
Yield: 12 medium-sized puffs

¼ cup butter	½ cup sifted all-purpose flour
½ cup boiling water	2 eggs

In a saucepan, add butter to boiling water. Continue heating until
butter melts. Add the flour all at once. Stir vigorously over heat until a ball
forms in center of saucepan.

Remove from heat. Add eggs, one at a time, beating the batter after
each egg is added. The batter should be very stiff.

Drop by rounded tablespoonfuls onto greased cookie sheet, leaving
about 1½″ between puffs.

Bake for 35 minutes. Remove to wire rack to cool. When cool make a
small opening ¾-way around puff, and fill with favorite filling.

If you are serving these as a cookie – to be eaten with the hands –
don't overfill them. They work best with a stiffly whipped cream filling
which you can delicately flavor with chocolate or liqueurs, or with a
traditional creamy custard filling.

Strawberry Whipped-Cream Filling

A very light summertime dessert that's also very elegant.
Serve these on a pretty platter garnished with halved
fresh strawberries (hull still on).

Preparation time: 10 minutes
Yield: filling for 20 small puffs

1	cup chilled whipping cream	¾	cup fresh strawberries, sliced
¼	cup powdered sugar, sifted	½	teaspoon vanilla extract

Chill bowl, beaters and cream. Whip cream with sifted powdered sugar and vanilla extract until stiff.

Fold in sliced strawberries

Put a generous teaspoon of creamed filling into each puff so that filling shows between top and bottom halves of puff. Refrigerate or serve immediately.

Favorite Mandel Broit

These mildly flavored, toast-like cookies are favorites at breakfast, lunch, or late-night snack.

Preparation time: 35 minutes
Pan: cookie sheets, greased
Oven: 375°F. loaves for 15 to 20 minutes, slices for 20 minutes more
Yield: 60 cookies

1	cup vegetable shortening	4	cups flour
1	cup granulated sugar	1	teaspoon baking powder
4	eggs	½	cup nuts, chopped
1	teaspoon vanilla extract		(optional)

Preheat oven to 375°F.

In a large bowl, cream together the shortening and granulated sugar. Add the eggs and vanilla extract. Mix well and set aside.

Sift the flour and baking powder together and add gradually to the creamed mixture. Add nuts and mix very well.

Knead the dough on a lightly floured board. Divide dough into five or six separate rolls about one inch high and 2½ to 3 inches long. Bake rolls on greased cookie sheets for 15 to 20 minutes, until browned.

Remove rolls from oven and slice into pieces, one inch wide. Place slices cut side down and bake another 20 minutes, turning slices after 10 minutes so both sides are lightly browned and crisp.

Remove slices to wire rack to cool.

Variations: You may substitute almond extract for vanilla extract. Add candied fruits instead of nuts, if you wish.

Index